the Grandma book

Editor: *Ruth Benedict*

Production: *Sally Manich, Sue Flower, Jan Kumbier, Henry de Fiebre, Peggy Bjorkman*

International Standard Book Number: 0-89821-045-3
Library of Congress Catalog Card Number: 82-62528
©1982, Reiman Publications, Inc.,
5400 S. 60th Street, Greendale, Wisconsin 53129

CONTENTS

FROM MY KITCHEN WINDOW

In Farming, We Live by Faith
By *Wilma Shauers* 5

The Gift
By *B. Purkis* 5

Farming's Made a Good Life
By *Verda Welch* 6

Soup, Like Love, Warms the Coldest Heart
By *Elizabeth Van Steenwyk* 7

Fresh Furrows Display His Faith
By *Rachel Erb* 8

Twilight Moments Stir Up Bright Hope
By *Bernice Maddux* 9

The Old Swing Was a Place for Dreamin'
By *Shirley Peterson Brander* 10

Memories Return as We Two Retire
By *Mary M. Porterfield* 10

Childhood Days
By *Leona Wiltse* 11

Haying...and a Light Heart
By *Mary Noble* 12

Fruit Room Shows Life's Worth Living
By *Barbara Huff* 13

I REMEMBER WHEN...

Old Country School Set Life's Stage for Us
By *Irene Madden* 15

Nothing Could Top Those Old Cattle Drives
By *Lorraine Kaitfors* 16

You Just Didn't Cook Without an Apron!
By *Virginia Hearn Machir* 18

First Sewing Lesson Taught More than Stitches
By *Mary K. Arthur* 20

Light-as-Chiffon Hopes Rested on Pie Supper
By *Kate Lewis* 21

Like Mama, Her Old Scissors Were Something
Special, By *Joyce Whitis* 22

Life Revolved Around the Water Pump
By *Nancy Burcham* 23

Mama's Cornmeal Mush 24

Remember the Taste of Home-Smoked Hams?
By *Helena K. Stefanski* 25

Fields Seemed Endless While Hoeing Dad's Corn
By *Katherine Twomey* 27

Barney...One Very Special Horse
By *Elsie Boyd* 28

A Daughter All Her Life
By *Helena K. Stefanski* 29

Pulling Mints Was Our Winter Fun
By *Ruth Moose* 30

Summer Was Fun at the Bendin' Tree
By *Ruth Williamson Harden* 31

To Grandma, They Were "Receipts"
By *Charlotte Lanham* 32

Those Old-Time Ailments Had Nasty Cures!
By *Sara Brandon* 34

Yesterday's Cures Were Just Unbelievable!
By *Lee Duncan* 35

Threshing Day Made Summer Complete
By *Madolyn Brown* 36

Mysterious Gift Meant So Much to Her
By *Kathy Gray* 38

Thank Goodness for Toasty Featherbeds!
By *Zoe Rexroad* 40

Autograph Book Brings Back Memories
By *Margaret Buell Allen* 41

Saturday Night Meant Well-Earned Fun!
By *Elaine Derendinger* 42

Grandma's Cooking Heritage Rested at Noodle
Table, By *Linda Inman* 43

Nobody Missed Out on Sunday's Family Dinner
By *Helen Rawlings* 44

BLEST BE THE TIE THAT BINDS

Chickens Taught About Love and Caring
By *Marjorie Burris* 47

Ode to My Cookbook
By *Bethene Larson* 48

These Hands Have Tender Strength
By *Katie Keehner* 49

Everybody Loved Aunt Nanny's Peonies
By *Jean Foster* 50

A Lifetime of Tenderness Shows in Her Hands
By *Berna Dean Kofoot* 51

She Left a Legacy of Love and Pepper Relish
By *Betty Jane Hewitt* 52

His Hands Have Quiet, Loving Strength
By *Marjory Scheufler* 52

Her Love Lives on in All of Us
By *Elaine Taylor* 53

She Had Her Eye on Farmer for a Beau
By *Carolyn Owens* 54

Life Goes On, and That's Just Beautiful
By *Lila Allen* 54

NATURE AT MY DOORSTEP

Will the Swallows Come Back to Clark's Dairy?
By *Rosalie Clark* 57

Morning Starlight Softens a Harsh Mood
By *Frances Armstrong* 58

Take Time—Enjoy Life's Glories
By *Shirley Harvey* 59

Each Dawn Holds Promise for the Future
By *Diane Lane* 60

Bittersweet Autumn Cannot Linger
By *Bernice Maddux* 62

Each Month Is Rare and Precious
By *Marlyce Peterson* 63

Spring in the Garden
By *Ruth Hale Woodside* 64

1

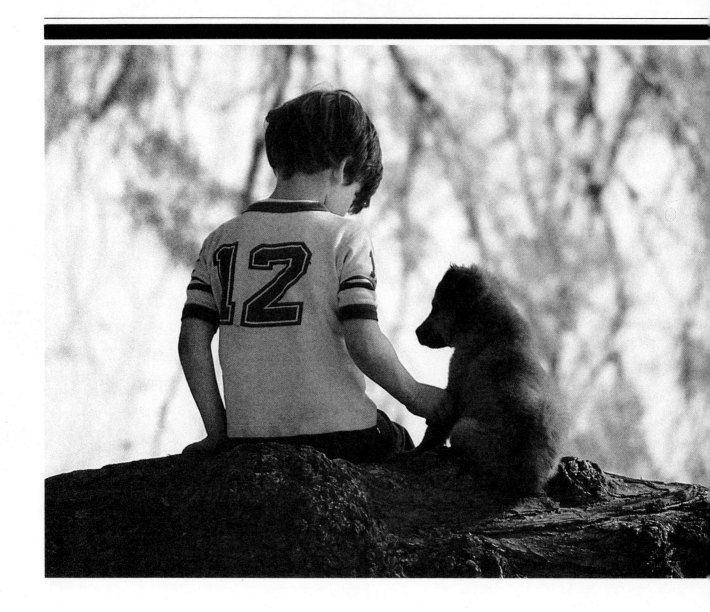

From My Kitchen Window
Reflections on a Good Life

In Farming, We Live By Faith

By *Wilma Shauers of Beeler, Kansas*

Heavy rains flooded our creek during the night, catching two old cows and their calves on the opposite side.

When we started feeding this morning, the old cows eased into the water and came swimming across. After some hesitation one calf followed; but the other could not bring himself to step into the water. He spent 10 minutes bawling and running frantically back and forth.

Finally he backed up and took a running leap, plainly expecting to clear 10 feet of water in one jump. When he hit the water, he went completely out of sight, but came up headed in the right direction and swimming strongly.

Watching him I thought how much time we farmers waste in worrying. Surely no one segment of our population faces more uncertainties and frustrations that are beyond its control. Weather and weeds, insects and diseases, government rulings, soaring expenses—the list is endless and we fret hours over them, individually and collectively.

We worry over the right time to plant wheat, will it come up, will it winter over, what price we'll get for it. We spray it and buy hail insurance and get all steamed up about harvest.

Eventually the wheat is harvested, and we like to feel our stewing and fretting is what brought the crop in. But deep down inside, beneath the worry, a farmer knows there is a mystery to his business.

Whether he is hailed out or brings in a bumper crop, much of the worrying is for naught. Things will be as they will be.

Just as the calf knew by instinct he could swim, so we must learn to accept the unknown working of things beyond our control. The very act of farming is an act of faith.

NATURE *has its own song to sing.*
We need to learn to accept
the unknown working of things
beyond our control.

The Gift

When I was a child were the skies as blue?
Were the clouds as puffy and white?
Were the sunsets of such a magnificent hue?
The birds' song such pure delight?
Did the years of living help me to see

The beauty of the flowers?
Is growing old the magic key
That gives value to the hours?

—B. Purkis of Edmonton, Alberta

Farming's Made a Good Life

By Verda Welch of Corinne, Utah

The years have rolled by since my husband and our sons operated our farm, and I live alone now, but still on the farm. I still feel farming was and is a good way of life for a family.

I remember sitting on the back steps in the cool of the evening, listening to the hum of the milking machines in the barn and the croaking of the frogs in the nearby ditch. The day, not unlike the season, had not quite lived up to our expectations, but the good had far outweighed the bad, and I was content.

The spring and summer, with their promises of hope, had been fulfilled, and the gold-and-green-checkered fields stretching out before me were part of the miracle of life and growth. I sensed an awareness of God's hand in winter snows, summer sun, the rains and natural rivers, joining man in the construction of reservoirs, dams and canals that water might flow where and when needed.

We found therapy in our flowerbeds and vegetable garden. The soil contained life and promise. Our labor in it gave birth to dreams and solutions to problems.

Sometimes I was thankful for the work and responsibilities which kept our sons home most of the evenings. They were too tired to go out for an evening of entertainment, and I was too tired to lie awake worrying about a possible accident if they were not home at the time I thought they should be.

Under their father's guidance I saw them learn how to plow a straight furrow, plant a row, string a tight fence and build proud stacks of hay. They learned the merit of honest labor and the value of earned money. Their 4-H clubs gave

THERE'S a promise of life in each day in the country...and working there preserves what's good.

hem incentives to care for the exhibit products
it the fairs. A blue ribbon was worth all the
:ffort the enterprise had cost.

If the promised vacations were sometimes
swallowed up in the summer's work or
disappointments, there was hope that next year's
plans would materialize.

The planning, sharing, building and
playing together strengthened our family and
built many happy memories for the future. The
disagreements were short-lived and unimportant.
The disappointments and discouragements, which
at times whispered that the toll was too heavy,
were forgotten when troubles were over and life
again flowed smoother.

I feel it is still a good way of life, and I
agre with the words of Rev. William O. Rogers in
his "Meditations of a Minister":

*"A tiller of the soil can more easily glorify his
work then almost anyone else. He orders the powers
of nature and sees them obey him. He lays his hand
on the earth and unseen forces become his servants.
His labors feed the hungry and clothe the needy.
His superintendent is the Omnipotent Creator, and
he works in partnership with the Divine.
His work is not a job, but a calling."*

Soup, Like Love, Warms the Coldest Heart

By Elizabeth Van Steenwyk of San Marino, California

Cookbooks from any country in the world have
at least one chapter devoted to the making
of soup. There are meat soups, chicken and
dumpling soups and vegetable soups with
emphasis on one particular lentil (depending on
that particular land).

Soup making is truly an art, as any good
cook knows, although the mysteries of its making
are not so much literary as intuitive. Just like all
meaningful things in life, soup is primarily a
creation of love.

Ask anyone over 30 about her first
remembrances of soup and her eyes will glaze
over with a backward look as she plugs into her
memory bank and calls forth visions of an over-
sized black kettle bubbling on the back of the
stove with a heavenly, overpowering fragrance.

In those remembered days, mother or
grandmother began with a soup bone (free from
farm or the butcher), onions, seasoning and
vegetables left over from the day before. Nothing
was wasted. Ever. Tired old potatoes, unpalatable
peas, woody turnips—all became delicious morsels
of nourishment, delightfully revived in a rich,
thick broth. They were leftovers, given a second
chance for accomplishment.

With these memories in mind, I ventured
forth on a soup-making expedition not long ago.
I bought a soup bone (no longer free), fussed at it
in my own still-shiny kettle (the patina of age will
come) and cautiously threw in the leftovers of the
week. At first, the modern children at my house
were aghast. Soup that doesn't come from a can?
Without a label?

"Try it, you'll like it," I urged, and soon
they became as children everywhere. I had found
my place in their memory banks. Soup, the
homemade kind, has already become a tradition
to my mod generation.

Now the kids rush in from school as I did
once and my mother before me, to lift the lid of
the pot on the back of the stove and sniff the
contents appreciatively.

The carrots that didn't quite make it, the
limas left from yesterday's dinner and the last
tomato from the vine, all take on new dimen-
sions. A second chance for my leftovers.

I thought about that the other day as I
pared and chopped and added to my newest soup.

And I thought how nice it would be if the
leftovers of our daily lives, our good intentions,
could be tossed into a similar pot simmering on
the back of the stove. A second chance to do
good. How nice. How convenient.

Into it would go the consoling note we'd

intended to write to a friend suffering the loss of a loved one, the encouraging smile we'd meant to give that lonely senior citizen sitting alone at home or the reassuring handclasp or pat on the back to the person we scarcely know at church.

Into this healing brew would go the visit to a critically ill friend in the hospital. How nice and convenient it would be if we had such a pot for all our leftovers—the acts of caring we never quite get around to performing—to save for a more convenient time.

But then I realized how wrong that would be and how fortunate we are that life does not provide us with a collecting vessel for our good intentions.

There's no second chance for a friendly smile or an encouraging word once the moment of giving is gone.

"Procrastination is the thief of time," Edward Young, the English poet said. It's the thief of our well-meaning acts, too, for the magic moment of sharing our concern for others is now, this moment, not an hour from now, or a week from now. Now.

Good intentions should not be simmered as a good soup. Good intentions are never better warmed over. The only ingredient good soup and good intentions have in common is love.

Fresh Furrows Display His Faith

By Rachel Erb of Milton, Pennsylvania

Here on the slope where I am disking ground, I can watch my husband turning furrows nearby. He's a farmer at heart and is enjoying his task.

As we work I'm thinking...how is it that a farmer gets excited each spring about plowing and planting? After all, it's the same old ground turned over, worked down and planted anew.

The same old ground, Ah, yes, but it's a new year! There are new expectations, new possibilities. A man in contact with the soil sees only the great potential, and cheerfully performs his part in converting that available potential into bountiful harvests. He's expecting the best, and would be very disappointed were there no fruits from his labors.

My thoughts turn upward to the Master Farmer. So many times He has patiently cultivated in my life and the fruits were meager. In humility I can only say, "Dear Lord, forgive." He tries again with each of us. The same old person, touched by His tender hand, can do so much.

HOW is it a farmer gets excited about plowing and planting each spring?

Twilight Moments Stir Up Bright Hope

By Bernice Maddux of Weatherford, Texas

No matter what remains to be done inside the house, at twilight I always hang up my apron and escape to the delightful freedom outside. Pretending to weed a flower bed or prune the unruly roses gives me an excuse for being there—if I should need one.

Like a rebel kite that has won its battle, my spirit soars into the evening air. Frustrations melt into nothingness and the day's cares all disappear.

Spending this twilight hour indoors must be a direct violation of the laws of nature…at least for me it is.

As I move quietly in the tiny strand of day remaining, I feel embraced by the sun, which clings stubbornly to the western horizon. Its slender pink fingers send the sun's last warm rays to my bare arms.

Within a hoe handle's length from me, quite undisturbed by any activity I might be engaged in, mockingbirds supper on grasshoppers, who have, in turn, suppered on our lawn, still limp from the heat of the afternoon sun.

Teased by the perfume of rose and honeysuckle blossoms, my senses dance frivolously with special freedom. I sit for a time on the porch steps, appraising the changes since yesterday's inspection.

And, if I am still enough, a hummingbird will ignore me as he drinks red juice from a blossom above me.

From a neighboring farm, a peacock broadcasts a proud "good-night" to his waiting mate and to the hushed world. Her answer comes clearly through above the animated baritone of bullfrogs perched on the cracked banks of the old dirt tank. The locusts raise a never-ending medley from the treetops.

Refusing to stop singing simply because of the absence of day, an assortment of birds happily harmonizes, while the bobwhite tries in vain to upstage them. Our only squirrel hops happily from limb to limb.

My English ivy seems to cast a pleased glance backward at the day's climb across the wall. A sprinkling of sparrows holds a talkfest among the ivy's majestic leaves and stereophonically I hear our tiny stream bubbling as it follows the downward curves of the rocky hill.

The light is fading as the sun travels farther down its path, but I can still see two rabbits silhouetted in its bronze afterglow. They see but think they are not seen. I watched the very pregnant one today with interest and mixed emotions, as she played havoc with our lawn to ready her bassinet.

The temptation to eavesdrop is overwhelming and I listen as brisk evening breezes seem to rustle with the intimate whispers of eager fireflies in the falling darkness.

A soothing rustle of oak leaves adds its welcome contribution to my reverie, while gently swaying baskets of fern, fantasia and brilliant begonia wave to me.

Glancing upward, I see shy marshmallowy clouds lifting billowy skirts to tiptoe across a placid sky, as if "hide-and-seeking" with a playful breeze.

I observe that a multitude of baby frogs has homesteaded on our patio for the night. I'm amused at the efforts of a male redbird perched on the now-still water sprinkler as he tries to scold it into giving him just one more cooling shower.

Snuggled between the light and the darkness, this special blend of lingering day and falling night intrigues and mystifies me. It is here I come closest to God and my island of peace. And I offer a prayer of thanksgiving for what's right with the world.

So many things are.

When the sun has gone, I can't imagine that any future sunset could possibly be so beautiful. But I know there will be more. A dove coos in the distance as I close the yard gate and make my way inside.

The Old Swing
Was a Place for Dreamin'

By Shirley Peterson Brander of Green Bay, Wisconsin

The old swing had its own corner of the farmyard, sheltered by two large spruce trees. It stood between the overgrown patch of tiger lilies and the bridal wreath bush. I discovered early in my life that in the bright sunshine of a summer afternoon there was no place like it.

The swing seemed to have always been there, though worn and weakened parts had been replaced from time to time.

Unlike the cold steel pipes and harsh chains of modern swings, our swing's warm ropes invited me to sit and pass some time…and the hand-fashioned wooden seat opened its lap to me for a comforting rock.

I could sit there for long afternoons, looking down at the tracks my dragging feet made in the dusty pit below the swing's arc. I could trace designs in the sand with a stick and then challenge myself to swing back and forth without disturbing the artistic patterns I had created.

If I held the ropes tightly and laid back as far as I could, there was a world of nothing but treetops and blue sky to see.

From my vantage point on that old swing I could view my world—not only the immediate world of home and family but also the world which required only a little dreaming to visit.

In my dreams I planned my brilliant future. There were so many thoughts to be sorted in my mind!

If anyone had asked me what I was doing sitting there alone I would have answered "Nothing."

But inside me there were dozens of problems being solved and a host of dreams being shaped.

Unlike the subtle and quiet colors of my old swing, today's noisy, striped, cold, steel swing sets demand attention. So instead of contemplating the fullness of life, one is drawn to consider the endless swirl of color winding around the gaudy supports.

And with two fancy swings, a glider and a monkey bar crying out for companionship, there's no appeal or room for solitary contemplation.

Maybe we need the flexible ropes and the familiar seat of an old-fashioned, farmyard swing to bring us full circle and back to ourselves …content and free.

Memories Return
As We Two Retire

By Mary M. Porterfield of Payson, Arizona

Living on a farm, working alongside your husband, makes you familiar with the labor, sweat, dreams and love that go into the land.

There's a kinship that is difficult to put into words and even harder to explain to outsiders. With more than a half-century of farm living behind you, the day you begin your retirement tells you how much you have to love farming to farm.

When you walk your land for the last time and see the little places only God and you know about, the knolls, the ditches, the wet spots you'd like to tile someday, and you see the improvement it made to clean up a fence row, you know a deep satisfaction.

You think about the time you found a killdeer's nest right over there near the rock pile. You tiptoed around that spot for days and kept your eyes on the progress of the four, gray-green eggs. Then one day a weasel found those eggs and you felt the sorrow and despair of your frantic little feathered friend.

You remember the opening in the woodlot where the doe stood with her wobbly legged fawn. It could scarcely stand, but hungry, it nudged its mother for nourishment.

There were times when you observed creatures of the woods drinking from the ditches. Wild animals and birds were not afraid of you on the tractor. Red-winged blackbirds swooped so close you could almost reach out and touch them.

You walk in another field and remember the nights the thunder rumbled and flashes of lightning lit up the sky, the times you both worked until dawn getting fragrant bales of hay into the barn. There were times you thought you could get in "just one more round" before a storm but you didn't quite make it.

You were pelted with hail or thoroughly drenched before you found shelter under the hickory nut tree or raced down the narrow lane to the pole barn. But in the end you laughed.

There isn't a field on the whole farm you can think of that hasn't been the setting for an impromtu lunch or supper. Sometimes it was a complete meal with folding table and all the trimmings. Other times, dinner was served on the tailgate of the pickup amid bags of fertilizer and seed, with sandwiches and cold beans on the menu.

And now the time has come when you must leave it all—the labor, sweat, dreams and love of the land.

You sense that the family moving in after you will experience many of the same things you have.

They will struggle from dawn to dark, working with nature at terrific odds. They will guzzle gallons of water while working in the blistering sun and gulp hot coffee from a thermos to ward off shivers on windy winter mornings.

They will share dreams of fixing, changing and improving their land. And, they'll go right on living it whether their crops fail or not.

That's your comfort, leaving your land with another dedicated farm family. Now you can gather your memories and turn your faces toward the next adventure of living in your autumn years.

Childhood Days

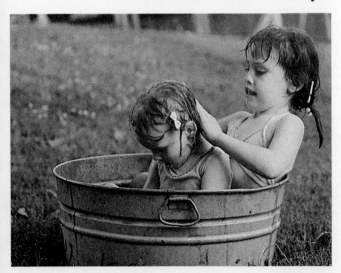

Now that I'm growing old,
I can be really bold
And tell of things that used to be—
A childhood so gay and so free.
How many crawdads I seined from the creek,
How many trees climbed where little birds cheep,
How many puddles I waded after a rain.
How many clover flowers made into a chain.
How many marbles made of shale.
How many berries picked in a pail.
How many rows of corn I hoed, on a horse-drawn
*   cultivator I rode.*
Drove a team of horses to pull a load of hay—
*   loosely it was piled; not baled as today.*
Only the memories remain; now I share with the
*   grandchildren sitting by my chair.*

—Leona Wiltse of Altoona, Kansas

11

Aunt Saidy at the Organ

You should hear Aunt Saidy at the organ—
* her rendering brings tears to my eyes.*
As she battles those old loved hymns, you can hear
* the tortured cries of the notes of the dear old organ*
As Aunt Saidy strives for the tune;
She's taken lessons for 20 years—
I hope she learns them soon.

You should listen to Aunt Saidy singing, such
* glory in a voice so sandpaper fine.*
Combined with a few notes copied from a bullfrog,
* her songs recall aspirins to mind.*
When Aunt Hester tunes up her fiddle,

and joins in with Aunt Saidy at the keys,
* it puts all the screech owls of the forest to shame*
* with their enthusiastic melodies.*

And our ol' hound dog always joins them whenever
* they play and sing their songs.*
His sad yodeling complements them greatly,
* for he can hold those high notes so long.*
What a wonderful, cultured concert I'm hearing;
* such a privilege to hear such talented folks.*
Pass me an Alka-Seltzer cocktail at intermission
to calm all this emotion their harmonizing evokes.

—Cora Harrison of Ruffin, South Carolina

Haying...
And a Light Heart

By Mary Noble of Edwards, New York

As I drive through the country on a sunny day in June and see farm tractors working in a hayfield, I get a homesick feeling, especially if I see a woman at the wheel of one of the tractors.

When we retired from farming 9 years ago my husband and I bought a house in the village just down the road. So I am still near my roots.

There were some things about spending 6 to 8 hours on a tractor that weren't pleasant, like the sunburn that resulted from wearing shorts and forgetting to take along slacks to put on after the legs had taken all the sun they could stand.

And there was the lameness that came from sitting so long without a change of position. The left knee might get especially painful if the work required that I use the clutch a lot. Sometimes the sun would be almost unbearably hot, and my desire for a drink of ice water was overwhelming.

Still I get that feeling that I am missing

something good when haying season comes around every summer. Like the days when I was sent to the back 10-acre meadow to rake or bale.

It was out of sight of the farm buildings and the highway, nestled down between the hills and rocks of our back pasture. The meadow was flat and almost square, so I didn't have to concentrate too much on my driving. That was where I could really enjoy myself.

I could daydream to my heart's content, think about the past, the present and the future. Many problems were solved out there, at least in my mind. I could sing at the top of my voice with no one to criticize or ridicule. (Sometimes I could hardly hear myself over the noise of the tractor motor!)

The only living beings were the birds and an occasional woodchuck that popped up from its hole and then ducked down again as I approached.

There was a wonderful feeling of freedom in the 10-acre meadow, and that is what I miss most of all every summer.

Fruit Room Shows Life's Worth Living

By Barbara Huff of Broomfield, Colorado

The harvest is now past and already we've experienced a few light snowfalls. For me this is a brief period of reflection on the busy months behind us and for regrouping my energies for the push before the holidays. Soon we'll be closing another year.

I've taken a little time to wash some curtains and to clean some neglected closets. I spent several hours one day sorting some things in our storeroom, which also serves as our fruit closet.

I enjoy lingering in that room. All the jars of fruit stand on the shelves like trophies of my hard work and frugality.

So much of what we farm wives do each day never shows, so that makes my fruit collection especially meaningful to me.

At the end of each day the house seems messier than it was before I cleaned it. The beautiful meals I've prepared have been devoured and there's not a crumb left to show for my efforts. So many of my daily tasks on the farm are done only to be redone before the sun sets on another day.

But that's why I enjoy lingering in my fruit closet. There stands tangible proof that I've been busy and accomplished something. Telephone conversations don't show, and within a half hour, neither do mopped floors.

But my freezer is groaning from the bounties of the recent harvest and the shelves are sagging from the wonderful weight of my accomplishments.

I wonder what else shows in my daily life? Is there a light shining in my eyes which is a reflection of God? Is there a calmness in my daily living which has come from appreciating the promises of life? And what about my wrinkles— are they scowl lines or smile lines?

It seems to me, that when you really stop to think about it, everything we do shows in one way or another.

It's a message we all need to remember.

13

2

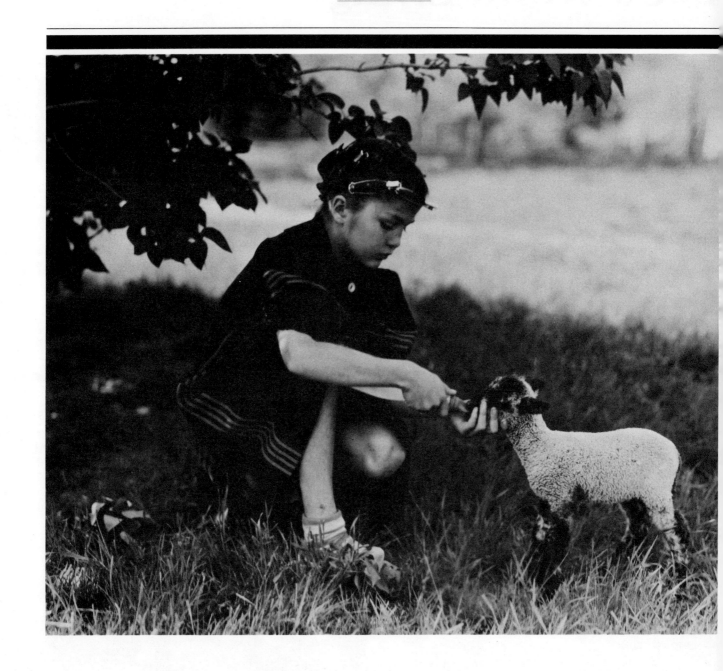

I Remember When...
Looking Back on Yesterday

Old Country School Set Life's Stage for Us

By Irene Madden of Thayer, Missouri

Growing up on a farm just north of Thayer, Missouri gave me a chance to begin my education in a one-room school. It was my classroom for 8 happy, enjoyable years.

There were no buses to our little Kings Point Elementary, only those to take those past eighth grade into town to high school.

So we all walked to school. My brothers and sisters and I walked 1 mile to and from school. Several others walked a longer distance. The walk through this beautiful country was always a lot of fun. My sister and I usually ran most of the way so we could join the boys in playing ball before the 8 a.m. bell rang.

None of us seemed to mind the walk, except during snowy days. Very few children had boots then, so a burlap sack from the barn was cut into wide strips and wrapped around our feet to keep the snow off our shoes.

Our teacher was usually up early and there before us and had the fire built and the building warm. In the winter months children walking the farthest were dismissed early to get home before it was too cold and dark.

I can remember how many days in winter we would run home to the smell of good, fresh pork, for it was butchering time. Several of the neighbors had gathered to help Daddy butcher.

Most of the time we were dismissed from school at 4 p.m. It was always sad to me when school was cut in April, because you didn't see the other children until classes began in August. I can still smell that little schoolroom when we entered the first day—scrubbed spotless and smelling like new lead pencils.

Our water came from a well on the schoolgrounds and was drawn with a bucket and a chain. When we were thirsty, we lined up and drank from the same cup (and hardly ever got a cold).

One memory that stays with me is when we lined up out in front of the school and pledged allegiance to our flag. I still get chills of excitement thinking about it!

Christmas at school was such a happy time. We began working on our program in late November and the teacher dismissed classes at 2:30 so we could work on our program again un-

SPECIAL friendships were sealed forever at the old, one-room country schoolhouse.

til 4. On the day of the program, most of the mothers came. Few fathers did, as most everyone made a living by farming and it was very hard for the menfolk to get away.

We had some wonderful teachers at that one-room school. One teacher taught all eight grades, working very hard during class hours. The teacher always went to the playground with us at recess time for a wonderful, playful 15 minutes.

When I was in sixth grade my teacher had us memorize the 48 states and the capitals. To this day I still remember them all. She was a good teacher—if she said do something, she meant for you to do it!

There were never any parents at school, because a teacher corrected the children. In those days at school, the teachers were in complete control.

On Friday afternoons, we had spelling bees, arithmetic matches or geography matches. And it seemed then that Kansas City, Missouri was a million miles away.

In April we had our "Last Day of School Picnic". The mothers all came carrying picnic lunches—it was a fun day, although a little sad, for some of us really loved school!

How nice it would be if everyone could know the real joy of country living *and* attending a one-room school for just 1 month!

Nothing Could Top Those Old Cattle Drives

By Lorraine Kaitfors of Prairie City, South Dakota

One of my fondest memories of growing up is about the old-time cattle drives when the cowboys would drive their cattle to the railroad along the dusty roads through the rangeland.

My parents lived by the main road so all the cowboys coming up from the south made our place one of their regular nightly stopovers. Their herds covered 15 to 20 miles per day—in good weather and with good luck.

When I was growing up all the ranges had been fenced. The cattle were moved sometimes through private pastures, but mostly along the main road, since this was the shortest and easiest route, and water and grazing were available at all of the ranches along the way.

Since there were no phones, we never knew when a cattle drive was coming through until the "point" rider appeared at the door to ask if it was alright to stop over and corral their cattle. He'd ask if they could feed and water their horses and ask Mother if she would prepare meals.

The point rider was always the one who came on ahead and gave us a couple hours' notice and a head count for supper.

No one was ever turned away...and I remember how my mother always bustled around to get supper for the cowboys.

We had a big hill behind our house, so I was always sent up to watch for the sight of the first cattle coming over the rise to the south so Mother could put the potatoes on to cook.

Soon we would hear the herd bawling and the voices of the riders as they moved the cattle steadily along the road. Usually one rider rode ahead to lead and direct the lead cows into the main gate of the ranch where they would spend the night.

I would almost "run my legs off" from the house to the hill and back—in a frenzy of excitement—to keep my mother informed of their progress.

After corraling the herd in our yard or a corner of our pasture, the men would take care of their horses—unsaddling, watering and feeding them, since it was the law of the trail that the needs of a man's horse were taken care of before his own.

Then the men would clean up at the water tank, washing off the trail dust as best they could. They'd sit outside the house, waiting to be called in for supper.

Since I was very small, I don't remember everything my mother served the cowboys but I do know there was always plenty to eat. There was homemade bread, home-churned butter, home-canned and cured meat, eggs, plenty of fresh vegetables, fruit, sugar cookies, doughnuts and other goodies. She was prepared.

I was never allowed to eat at the table with the cowboys...only my father, but I'm sure I never missed a move or word.

After supper the men would sit on the steps to smoke and discuss the day's adventures and sometimes they would sing. Most of the time they "hit the hay" early, bedding down in the barn or haystack near their horses and gear.

They would be moving out again at sunrise so I seldom got in on the breakfast scene, but I usually made it up in time to see them move out.

It was always a great disappointment to me when a big herd came along with a chuck wagon. Then the cowboys ate their meals on the trail and we wouldn't get to see much of them.

Once in a while one of the men's wives would be along to do the cooking and she would come in to visit with my mother for a while. Because of these cattle drives we got to know a lot of the men and their wives and welcomed their yearly visits.

I was always dreaming about going along on one of those trail drives...riding my own horse and camping out along the way. But by the time I was old enough, the trails were no more. Livestock was being moved by trucks and I missed out on the trail rides. I still feel a little bit cheated from one of life's most exciting adventures.

The drives were always made in late summer and early fall. Sometimes there would be

HOW kids used to dream about riding across the rangeland with those fascinating cowboys!

Cattle Drive...

two or three drives a week passing by our place.

As they neared town they grew larger because they often picked up small herds along the way. I can remember my father adding his cattle to a herd as it came by.

Now and then something would frighten the cattle at night—lightning, a coyote or anything—and it didn't take much if the herd was nervous and edgy. If the cattle stampeded, they instinctively ran for home. It often took hours for the cowboys to get them rounded up again.

Almost every herd had at least one "ornery critter" intent on causing trouble and being disagreeable, such as a renegade steer or wild cow determined to go back home. Sometimes the whole herd went astray.

My father sometimes went along on the train to the Chicago stockyards with the cattle because it was best to have someone go to look after them at the other end. He took turns with our neighbors going on that annual trip to the stockyards.

I remember my dad's excitement when it was his turn to go, with Mother getting out the old brown suitcase, and packing for him.

Dad's trip to Chicago was a great mystery to me because he got there on a train full of cattle and he rode in a thing called a caboose which was hooked on behind the cattle cars. How I wanted to go along!

When he came home he always brought Mother and me lovely gifts. I still have a string of green glass beads with tiny pink and yellow flowers on them that he brought my mother and a brown and white striped dress—size 5—that he brought me. My, they were beautiful and, of course, to me they still are very precious indeed.

My husband and I still live on my parents' place. When I climb that big hill behind the house, I can still see in my mind's eye the first of the cattle topping the rise, hear the bawling cattle and see the cowboys heading for the bedding grounds after a long day in the saddle.

You Just Didn't Cook Without an Apron!

By Virginia Hearn Machir of St. Charles, Missouri

Aprons make me an oddity in this space age. I prefer to protect myself from dribbles and splashes by wearing one. Most of my friends never use an apron.

Oh, perhaps someone gave them a froth of green organdy, embellished with a red poinsetta to don for chic entertaining during the holiday season. But for every day, they use a small towel buttoned to the handle of the refrigerator door, which they flick their fingers down occasionally.

But my grandmother wore aprons. She was a practical women who made her own, as did most women of the day. There was a set ritual about her day that began at 5 in the morning when she donned a huge, bibbed, blue-and-white-checked gingham apron kept on a hook behind the kitchen door.

As the morning progressed, the pockets bulged as she went from room to room. An embroidery hoop here, a ball of yarn there, a shoe buttonhook, or a stray button that had fallen from grandfather's shirt. Her apron pockets often held goodies for me—a piece of hard horehound candy, or a big red apple.

At noon the gingham apron was whisked off and replaced with a small, dainty apron of frilly organdy, or lace-trimmed percale. It was a small scrap of an apron but still provided protection for her flowered dress while she dished up the Southern fare of hot biscuits, ham and red-eye gravy. On Sundays, Grandma wore the fanciest apron she owned. Her supply was endless and included every color of the rainbow.

When the women in the neighborhood

18

went to a quilting bee, a church supper, an apple-butter making or a threshing dinner, each flaunted her newest and prettiest apron. There was as much exchanging of apron patterns as there was recipes for Jeff Davis pie and burnt caramel cake.

I've seen my grandmother use her apron as an emergency dust cloth, swishing it across table tops on her way to answering a knock on the door. She also used it to tote things…like bringing up apples from the cellar, eggs from the henhouse, newly hatched baby chicks from the nest and wood chips from the woodpile. I've even seen her run out and flap her apron, yelling, "Schoo, schoo," to scare off chicken hawks flying low over the chicken house. When I was a child I used her apron for a crying towel when I fell down and skinned my knees.

Men wore aprons too, back in my grandmother's day. I remember the black rubber apron the ice man wore, the ticking apron the cobbler wore, the heavy leather one the blacksmith wore and the big white apron the baker wore. Today you never see a man wearing an apron unless he's barbecuing ribs at a picnic.

Aprons are as old as the beginning of the world. When Adam and Eve aroused the wrath of God in the garden of Eden, they made themselves aprons of fig leaves. Mary, Queen of Scots, is said to have left over 100 aprons. In the reign of Queen Anne, aprons were richly embroidered and decorated, and the Queen herself wore one.

But do you think I can get my daughter to wear one? She says aprons went out with the horse and buggy and she doesn't care if Queen Anne wore one.

I admire my daughter very much. She is a good mother and homemaker, besides having her name on the door of an accounting office. I've told her about grandmother's aprons. I've done everything to convince her to wear one but to no avail. She thinks I'm unique because I wear an apron. Or does she secretly think I'm wierd?

When my 8-year-old grandson ties one of my aprons around his shoulders like a cape, and races around the lawn pretending he's Superman, I think the wedlock between the old-fashioned apron and the space age is complete.

FRIED chicken, rice pudding, or flapjacks, no cook worth her salt worked without an apron on.

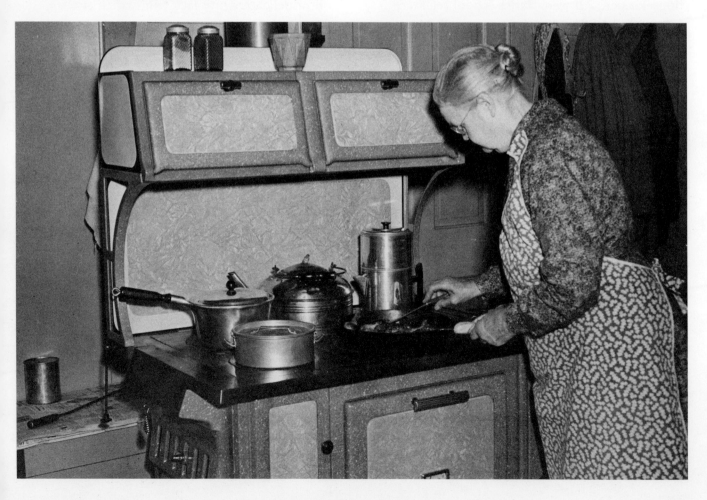

First Sewing Lesson Taught More than Stitches

By Mary K. Arthur of Oshkosh, Wisconsin

Many a Valentine's Day has come and gone since I was a fourth-grader at our little one-room schoolhouse in northeastern Wisconsin. Yet I have never forgotten that holiday, because a red heart pincushion made it special. I was delighted to find that little heart recently while unpacking a box of family keepsakes.

Our teacher was a tall, thin blond named Miss Zeinert. A strict disciplinarian, she possessed a special ability that made us eager to learn the three "Rs." Miss Zeinert had plenty to do—aside from teaching 40 youngsters in five grades, she acted as a mother, nursemaid and housekeeper. All were duties school teachers assumed in those days.

In the middle of January, the teacher announced some exciting news. On February 14th we would have a party and a contest for the most unique individual Valentine project. I could hardly wait to get home and tell my mother about the contest, knowing I could count on her teaching background for a clever idea!

Mother thought it was high time I learned the basics of sewing and suggested I make a heart-shaped pincushion. She said it could serve as my contest project and, later on, be a useful sewing accessory.

The school days to follow were filled with the excitement of party preparations. We fashioned a big cardboard mailbox for our Valentine exchange and designed elaborate cards for our mothers out of red construction paper and lacy white doilies. I volunteered to be on the refreshment committee and agreed to bring cookies.

On the Saturday morning before the party we sat at the kitchen table and Mother cut out a heart-shaped pattern from a piece of cardboard. I traced the pattern twice onto red cotton material and carefully cut around the cloth heart. Mother pinned them, right sides together. Next, she showed me how to thread a needle and stitch a seam by hand following the pin guides.

It was slow, tedious work for my little fingers and, when I finally finished, Mother realized there was no way to turn it right-side out. I didn't look up at Grandma, who had been quietly observing our progress. I knew her eyes were rolled heavenward, but at least she had the decency not to snicker.

Mother snipped a portion of the seam open and we turned the heart to the correct side. We stuffed it with several of Grandma's old silk stockings and I sewed the seam shut once again. That was when I noticed a tiny hole in the fabric! Mother had accidently cut a piece of the cloth when she opened the original seam.

Grandma smiled, shook her head and left the room, only to return moments later with a roll of delicate white lace trim which she suggested we sew around the seam to camouflage the flaw. Next, we attached a perky white satin bow to the middle of the heart. I was absolutely elated with the elegant pincushion and immensely proud of my newly acquired talent for sewing!

That afternoon, Grandma and I made my favorite meringue cookies. We frosted them with her best butter icing and trimmed each pink puff with a cinnamon heart.

It seemed like an eternity until the big day finally dawned. There was such excitement on Valentine's Day morning that no one paid much attention to lesson plans. Right after lunch, the party got under way. Everyone lined up and the teacher explained how we should judge the entries—we should vote for a winner from each class.

Some of the projects were really unique. There were clever Valentine posters, trimmed with red and white paper cutouts and shiny cherry suckers and handmade clay heart paperweights, decorated with macaroni "jewels."

One of the older boys entered a heart-shaped dish he had carved from a bar of soap.

Miss Zeinert tallied the ballots while we exchanged our cards. There were groans and giggles, whispers and shrieks as we read aloud our stacks of Valentine "mail."

Soon it was time for refreshments. When everyone was finally seated with their treats, Miss Zeinert announced the contest winners, starting with the first grade. I held my breath because the fourth grade competition was stiff. As all six of us crossed our fingers, the teacher called out Donna's name.

For an instant, I felt a surge of disappointment but Donna's enthusiasm was so contagious it rubbed off on all of us. She was the oldest child of a large family and I wondered how Donna had found the time between chores and school to design her lovely dishtowel.

Fashioned of white flour sacking, it was adorned with numerous clusters of embroidered red hearts and edged with intricate crochet.

The party ended when the school bus arrived to take us home. Mother and Grandma were anxiously awaiting my return.

I kept the heart up in my bedroom at Grandma's suggestion and we shared her pincushion. It was she, of course, who took on the responsibility of furthering my seamstress skills and Grandma taught me to knit and crochet, as well.

My mother's teaching experience proved a valuable asset whenever I needed ideas for school projects, but the pincushion was the first and last time I would ask her to help with sewing. Eventually, the heart was wrapped in tissue and stored away—saved as a memory of my first sewing lesson and of a Valentine's Day I'll always remember.

Light-as-Chiffon Hopes Rested on Pie Supper

By Kate Lewis of Purcell, Oklahoma

Pie Supper! When I was a young girl, the announcement of an upcoming pie supper started a rash of excitement and preparation among all of us. In just a few short days our town's general store sold enough crepe paper to decorate Main Street.

"What design will I use? What colors? How much paper do I need?" we'd wonder aloud. (You'd think we were making paper pies instead of beautifying pie boxes!)

Each box had to be different and "eye-catching". It was supposed to be kept a secret from prospective buyers, but somehow our beaus always managed to find out which box to bid on. When one suitor's bidding became especially intense, it prompted all the other fellows to keep right on bidding, making him pay the highest price possible. Sometimes a whole summer's wages went for just one pie!

Naturally a young lady's pride would be wounded if her beau didn't pay whatever price it took to get her pie—sometimes we even found it convenient to let another fellow walk us home that night.

Making a beautiful box required many hours of work and all the talent and ingenuity each of us could muster. Like everyone else, I felt my pie box just had to be the prettiest one!

Putting the pie together came *after* I did some sleuthing to find out what my fellow's favorite flavor was. The crust had to be tender enough to melt in the mouth, yet it had to stay intact and cut like a dream under his fork. Such a pie demanded extreme finesse!

When the evening of the event arrived, each pie box was carried in, wrapped in newspaper for secrecy's sake. For all of us, it had been a busy day of pressing our ruffled dresses and fixing our hair with curling irons.

At the supper, the pies were carefully unwrapped and labeled with numbers—one for the buyer and the other to identify the pie. Plenty of times we girls would volunteer to work up front on the stage—an opportunity to display one's charms was never turned down! Sometimes we seemed busier than we really were.

There were always practical jokes at pie

suppers, even though the girl whose pie became the trick didn't enjoy it much. One friend of mine watched her pie sold at a price way beyond her beau's reach (bid up by his friends) and then passed over to the community laughingstock.

There were other tricks going on behind the stage curtains. Once a bidder claimed his pie and his girl and escorted her to a desk, both of them unsuspecting of anything at all.

When she lifted the lid to reveal her pie, it looked a little unfamiliar. But it was complete with a golden crust and a meringue, so she served up a piece, discovering her coconut pie had turned to chocolate—a *peculiar* shade of chocolate. To her chagrin and his dismay, when he took a bite he found his mouth full of mud. It was even flavored with vanilla—which helped it none!

The prime event of a pie supper was the selection of the prettiest girl at a penny a vote. With the nominees' names written on the chalkboard, a heated contest began. Every girl yearned and expected to get the prized box of

chocolates—everyone except me.

All through childhood I had been told how homely I was. With huge freckles, bright red hair and a bit too much weight, I felt very unattractive. But on pie supper day I tried my best. Hair curled and makeup applied, I stepped out wearing a neat-fitting dress. I was hopeful, but I knew that prize was a thousand miles beyond my reach.

One year I sat with the other girls, waiting for the chairman to close the contest and finally announce that year's winner.

As usual, there was a lot of whispering among us as the emcee talked about the "bevy of beauties" on hand. Each of us nervously glanced across the room to catch a wink from our parents.

But I was too excited to look away for long. "If I don't win this year, I probably never will," I said to myself. But before I knew it, I heard my name being called!

That was the happiest moment of my life! As I walked forward to get those chocolates, my image did an "about-face". Now I was Cinderella—glass slippers and all!

Like Mama, Her Old Scissors Were Something Special

By Joyce Whitis of Stephenville, Texas

They're just an old pair of barber scissors —no longer shiny, no longer very sharp, blades shorter than other barber scissors, kind of funny lookin', hard to sell at a flea market. And yet... I'd never part with them because they're the only pair I remember Mama ever having with her the later years.

Away back there, back when I was only 3 or 4, I remember those very scissors as they snipped, snipped around my ears on Saturday afternoons. Mama would put me on the tin cracker box in a cane bottom kitchen chair, fasten a duckin' towel around my neck with the

biggest safety pin she could find, and I'd squinch up my eyes to keep the hair out. She always gave me a Buster Brown and I always fussed. If it was warm weather, she'd put the chair and cracker box on the porch and that made cleaning up afterwards easier.

Mama always cut my hair—until I was in high school I guess, and I always hated it. I can still feel that hair scratching my neck and remember how the trimming of my bangs always got hair in my eyes.

"Come on, Joyce, time for a haircut." I felt like running away from home. But if I had, Mama would have found me and dragged me back so she could make me "look nice".

Mama cut my brother's hair too and

Dad's. I don't remember that either of them ever went to a barber shop until my brother was almost grown. She must have lost interest in cutting hair then because they started getting barbered in town and she used the scissors for other jobs like sewing.

There's just no telling how many dresses and blouses and skirts and slacks and slips and gowns that those old black scissors cut out. Since Mama made everything we wore, and since she sometimes designed her own patterns, and since she was forever cutting out something on the dining table after supper, those scissors often kept long and late hours.

I saw my mother repair just about anything around the house that broke with those scissors, including mending screens. I remember watching her cut out pieces of screen wire to sew into holes that had been ripped here and there. I've seen her use the same scissors to cut screen wire for fly swatters and even pieces of tin which she used to stop up mouse holes in the kitchen cabinets.

The scissors didn't always have short blades but how well I remember the day they got that way! I was playing with empty spools and Mama's machine attachments and the scissors while Mama peddled away at her old Singer. I remember sticking one point of the scissors in an extra maching shuttle...somehow one of the

blades snapped off!

I was horrified and tried to hide the scissors but finally had to drag them out. I was certain that there would be some harsh words my way but Dad looked them over and said, "I can fix that". He broke off the other blade and then filed the two down to match.

Once Mama found me sitting on the window seat getting ready to cut the curling tail of a stinging scorpion with those same scissors.

After the funeral, when we were going through Mama's things, we found those scissors in her purse where she had carried them for many years. There was no question in my mind about who should have them. I reached for the short-bladed scissors and told my sisters, "There are mine". They didn't contest my claim. In fact they didn't even remember about the scissors, or want them.

I wanted those old scissors for several reasons, the best of which is that like my mother and dad, they were hardly ever idle. Like my parents, they did inventive, creative and resourceful things and like the two people I loved so much, they never failed to do more than was expected.

Folks like that, as well as well-built tools, are harder and harder to find. I carry those scissors just to remind me that such things do still exist.

Life Revolved Around the Water Pump

By Nancy Burcham of Sullivan, Illinois

P personally, I feel everyone should, when very young, rely for a time on the water from an old cistern pump.

When I was a child, the cistern pump stood on our back porch. From that rusty pump, which was once painted red, a pipe ran down through the weathered floor to a deep-storage tank below. Metal drainpipes caught the rains

that fell on our house and smokehouse roofs and channeled the water along the eaves and across the ground to the cistern's storage depths.

In rainy seasons, when the cistern was overflowing with rainwater, Mom often handed a bucket to me and said, "Carry water to the chickens."

At the pump, I hooked the bucket's handle over the waterspout and pumped the handle up and down twice. Immediately, the water began to flow from the spout into the bucket. There was nothing to it, and I continued to pump at a leisurely pace.

During a summer drought, getting rainwater from the cistern was not such an easy task. When Dad handed two buckets to me and said, "You'll have to carry water to the cattle, because the creek ran dry," I wanted to run and hide.

But I didn't. Instead, I approached the pump on the porch with great trepidation. As I began pumping the handle up and down with one hand, I reached for the lard can sitting nearby, which was filled with precious "prime water'. I poured the water into the top of the pump and held my breath. "Work, please work," I silently pleaded, as I pumped the handle faster and faster.

At last, the water began trickling down from the spout into the bucket. I pumped on and on without stopping, even as I removed one bucket and filled the other, then filled the lard can with water for a prime the next time someone went to the pump for water. As I lugged water to the cattle, I breathlessly prayed for the rains to come and fill the cistern once more.

One night in June the old cistern pump, filled with water from recent rains, saved our humble home from destruction. We used gas lamps to light the house at night, because there was no electricity. I was 7 at the time, and I said to Dad, "May I pump the gas into the lamps tonight?"

"Sure," he replied. "Stand on a chair at the kitchen table and start pumping."

Mama's Cornmeal Mush

Golden and nutty, stick-to-your-ribs warm and tasty, Mama's cornmeal mush was a regular for most kids who walked off to school on frosty winter mornings years ago. For old-time's sake, here's the recipe:

1 cup white or yellow cornmeal
1/2 cup cold water
1 teaspoon salt
4 cups boiling water OR water and milk

Combine cornmeal, cold water and salt. In top of double boiler, place 4 cups boiling water; gradually stir in cornmeal mixture. Cook and stir the mush over quick heat for 2 to 3 minutes. Reduce heat, cover and steam 25 to 30 minutes, stirring frequently until mixture is thick. Serve with syrup or other choices.

As I pumped away, Dad turned on the control valve, lit a match and held it to the white-gauze filament. Suddenly the lamp exploded! Flames shot to the ceiling. Escaping gas sprayed onto the chair, the floor and the navy sailor dress I was wearing.

I jumped off the chair and dashed for the living room door, unaware that my entire back side was engulfed in flames. Dad leaped across the room, crushed me to the floor beneath him and smothered out the flames with his body.

In the meantime, Mom grabbed the burning lamp, dashed outside to the cistern and pumped the handle twice. Water gushed forth from the spout and put out the flames. Next Mom filled a bucket with water and darted back to the kitchen to douse all the flames.

On lazy days, when my sister and I had nothing better to do, we took off the cistern's porch-floor lid and, lying on our stomachs, looked down, down, down into the deep, dark hole. It was fun to see our reflections looking back at us as our heads hung over the opening.

"H-e-l-l-o," we would yell. And the cistern echoed back "H-e-l-l-o, h-e-l-l-o", over and over.

One day Mom came in from getting water at the cistern pump and said, "The water smells terrible. We can't use it. An animal must have drowned in the cistern." We all went out back and watched as Dad beamed a light across the water in the cistern tank. "There it is," he said. "A rat got in somehow and drowned. We'll have to drain the cistern and clean it."

Within the hour, neighbors came to help, and the cistern was siphoned dry. It was a tiring job, but at long last the cistern was clean. Soon the rains filled it again.

We didn't worry about using water so hard our bathing soap wouldn't get sudsy. And we had no reason to call the "Culligan man". Our water was, without a doubt, rainwater soft at the cistern pump.

When we were muddy, sweaty or caked with chaffs of hay, we didn't track into the house to wash up. We stopped at the cistern pump on the porch and washed off all the grime.

The day finally came when drillers tapped a deep well, and plumbers piped running water into our house. With a turn of the faucet, we had water in the kitchen and the bath.

With that turn of the faucet, the kinship between nature's rains and our daily needs faded. Gone were the days of pumping and priming and praying for rain at the old cistern pump; but the appropriate appreciation for water lingers on.

Remember the Taste Of Home-Smoked Hams?

By Helena K. Stefanski of Lakewood, Colorado

At high noon, darkness hung as heavy as midnight in that shed. It had no windows and the inside walls and ceiling were black from smoke. But it was intended to be that way—it was a country smokehouse built by my father on our Wyoming ranch in the early part of the century.

The dim interior of the smokehouse always held an aura of mystery for us children. For a few weeks in the late winter and early spring we saw activity around the smokehouse, but after that it stood closed and silent for the rest of the year.

Yet we knew in that short time it played a crucial role in getting the delicious smoky flavor into the rosy homemade hams and golden-colored bacon Mother placed on the table throughout the year.

Father planned well ahead for this home smoking. During February, when the weather was crisp and cold, he butchered two hogs he had been carefully feeding for months.

After allowing the butchered carcasses to chill thoroughly, he cut and trimmed them into hams, shoulders and bacon slabs. He placed them into a long wooden tub and covered them with brine. He added crushed cloves of garlic to the brine to give the meat a very delicate flavor of garlic. He let the meat cure for about a month.

When Father felt the curing was completed, he took the meat from the brine and scrubbed off the excess surface salt with a stiff brush and lukewarm water.

Then he ran several thicknesses of baling twine through each shank end to hang the meat for smoking. He ran a long stainless-steel wire through the bacon slabs, a few inches from the narrow end of each long piece, and tied loops of twine to the protruding ends of the wire. The wire kept the heavy slabs from curling as they hung during that long, slow smoking process.

Before starting the fire, Father let the hams, shoulders and bacon slabs hang in the cold smokehouse for about 24 hours.

Father's smokehouse was a frame shed about 8 feet tall and 8 feet square. It maintained good regulation of temperature and a good flow of smoke and air inside, yet allowed the excess smoke to seep out between the boards and around the door.

The floor was concrete with an opening at one side for the smoke trench. Several movable 2 x 4s rested on short racks on two sides of the inside walls, about 6 feet from the floor. The meat hung from hooks on these 2 x 4s.

Not all our neighbors had smokehouses of their own, so Father invited those who didn't to use ours if they wished. They gladly accepted, and Father usually generously tended the fire for them until their meat was ready.

While the meat was curing in the brine, Father walked through the woods along the river, searching for hardwood for the fire.

He started the fire early in the morning at the outer end of the 10-foot smoke trench. It was covered with a huge metal pipe cut in half lengthwise, which led up to the hole in the cement floor inside the shed. This outside fire allowed better control of the temperature inside and also reduced the fire hazard.

Father controlled the fire by placing a big piece of tin at the opening of the covered trench —he either increased or restricted the flow of air that fed the fire, making sure it burned slowly and evenly.

Because our smoked meat had to last through the hot summer without spoiling, it was smoked longer and at lower temperatures than meat to be eaten within a short period of time.

Some farmers allowed their fires to die during the night and would rebuild them again in the morning, but Father preferred to keep his going until the meat was done. While this meant getting up several times during the night, he didn't seem to mind. Medium-sized hams took 3 days and nights of smoking time. Bacon took only 48 hours.

The smoking and drying process preserved the meat and helped develop a tangy, smoky flavor. It also added a rich mahogany-brown color to the outside and a cherry red color to the ham.

After smoking was completed, Father allowed the meat to cool and then he transferred it to another shed where it was hung, secure from flies and insects.

When Mother needed ham or bacon she went to this shed. Leaving the door open for light, she would remove a ham or bacon slab from a hook, place it on a homemade butcher's block, saw off what she wanted and return the rest to the hook.

When families came to visit, my brother and I invited the children to explore the farm with us. We never failed to take them to see the smokehouse.

We opened the door and stood staring into the darkness inside, letting the pungent aroma of smoke and smoked hams envelop us.

"This is where we smoke our hams and bacon," I would inform them with a feeling of pride and importance. "Daddy says the smoke keeps the shed as sound and hard as steel. No termites will touch it as long as it is used. It will last longer than any other building on the farm."

Anyone who has tasted home-smoked hams and bacon will share my nostalgia for country smokehouses.

I hope farmers will put them back in use and farm women return to serving home-smoked meats. Commercially prepared ham and bacon just don't compare.

CERTAINLY not every memory of how things used to be conjures up a pleasant image of yesterday's everyday life. But Mama sure got the clothes clean—no matter how long it took!

Fields Seemed Endless While Hoeing Dad's Corn

By Katherine Twomey of Hot Springs, South Dakota

Along about June in the summertime there would come a day when father announced cheerfully at the evening meal, "Tomorrow the children can start hoeing the corn". This remark always produced stricken looks on the faces of brother and me, but sister Margaret, who liked all kinds of farm work, never winced at the prospect of hoeing corn.

In a time when most farmers considered the corn "laid by" as soon as it grew too tall to be cultivated mechanically, Dad still wanted his corn hoed. He felt that the work was a good and useful outlet for the energies of children, providing them with physical exercise and mental discipline, fresh air and even a small income—for he paid us a little.

On a balmy summer morning he would lead us, armed with our implements of attack, to the cornfield where the endless rows stood rustling softly in the gentle breeze, the long, dark-green leaves shining with dew.

"It's a good day to work," Dad would say, gazing fondly around at his acres. After all the years that have passed, I still find myself thinking, when I step outdoors on a soft summer morning with the sun starting up the eastern sky, "Dad would call this 'a good day to work'."

As a rule, Dad's cornfields were fairly close to a stretch of woodland, because his farm had been purchased for stock feeding rather than for general farming. The land had a mixture of pasture, woods and tillable fields.

Dad always mentioned (rather unnecessarily) that if we got tired we could sit in the shade of the grove to rest. He was not averse to our resting as long as we didn't do more resting than working. Dad almost always referred to a piece of woodland as a "grove" and frequently pointed out that the grove presented an attractive prospect to please us while we were working, as indeed it did.

To me, the proximity of the grove was more of a trial than a pleasure, for I would have much preferred to be wandering in the woods, scanning the branches for birds and poking about to see what was growing under the trees.

Each day we would scritch-scratch our way down the rows, sometimes nicking off a fine, healthy cornstalk, which we would hastily replant. We hoped it might root again but made sure, anyway, that it was less conspicuous standing up than lying down.

There was a feeling of accomplishment in arriving at the end of a pair of rows, even though that was partially offset by the necessity of starting back down another pair. We were sure the fields were at least a mile in length as we looked back through the long, long ribbons of green.

Dad, when questioned, explained that they were such-and-such number of rods. But the term meant nothing to us, whereas *everybody* knew that a mile was a very long distance.

Margaret, being older and more enthusiastic, inevitably traveled farther and faster, getting way ahead of brother and me. Not surprisingly, she was also paid more. Sometimes Dad released the younger two of us after the very welcome lunch hour, depending on the size of the field and the extent of the weed growth. And, I suspect, on how much wholesome mental discipline and physical exercise he thought we needed.

Father's interest in having the corn hoed was not generated solely as a method of child training. He really liked to have his corn hoed. In years when no children were available he would hire some workman in need of money and send him into the field.

One fine summer morning toward the end of an August, when Dad and Mother were driving toward town, they spotted an elderly man, hoe on his shoulder, walking down the road toward one of our fields.

Dad's expression was made up of surprise, chagrin and amusement as he exclaimed, "I'm afraid I know where he's going".

Dad had hired the man weeks earlier to hoe some corn and had forgotten all about him. The man, after collecting wages a couple of times, had proceeded to hoe on through the summer, disappearing into the corn rows every morning. Because the stalks were tall enough to hide him,

Dad never noticed that he was there.

Mother said if it hadn't been for that accidental sighting, the old man would have continued hoeing until he was overtaken by the corn pickers in the fall.

Dad paid the man and another summer in the corn ended—with the usual, beautiful harvest in the fall.

Barney...
One Very Special Horse

By Elsie Boyd

Barney's mother died when he was born in the spring of 1938, so he was raised on cows' milk—fed by means of a large bottle and an old rubber nipple. As a result of this close association with humans, the long-legged red colt grew into one of the biggest and most lovable pets we ever had on the farm.

During those early months his coat was a trifle rough and his stomach a little too large, but he soon began to thrive on his unusual diet. When grain and second-cut hay were added, he grew even faster than an ordinary horse.

We knew he had the blood of several different horse breeds mixed in his veins, so we were not surprised when big Clydesdale feet and strong Percheron muscles began to develop—forerunners of the powerful physique to follow.

For several years Barney's home was a nice box stall just inside the barn door in the winter, and an old shed in the pasture in warm weather. But he had such an attachment to people that he would come near the house whenever he could, either by coaxing someone to let him out for a time, or by managing to master the ways of gates all by himself.

He never outgrew his fondness for cows' milk—even full-grown he always tried to get a few swallows whenever he could. I remember one time when he was a yearling...my husband had carried a pail of milk to the house and set it on a

chair on the porch to be strained. A few minutes later I opened the front door and bumped into a horse's rump!

"Barney!" I scolded. But I was too late. He lifted a dripping-white muzzle from the pail to gaze at me with a "What's-the-matter?" look. I grabbed his mane and pulled his head aside—to discover that the 2 gallons of milk were all in his big stomach!

Barney was at all times a gentle horse, and when broken to harness was a patient and hard-working beast who needed no urging to do his best. And he always took it upon himself to see that his teammate worked well, too. During his 26 years he was teamed with several different horses, and if they were ever inclined to hold back on the job, they received nips and nudges from Barney until they threw their weight into the collar and pulled their share.

In Barney's younger days all the roads except a few of the main ones were just plain old mud. When the frost went out in the spring and the March rains came, there were many ruts and wily chuckholes for several weeks—posing all sorts of traps for the vehicles of unwary travelers.

The cars of our neighbors and other passersby, as well as our own, were often stuck during that time. There was an especially big mudhole near the end of our driveway, and the cry "Get Barney!" was often heard on the worst days.

The big horse knew exactly what to do and he relished doing it. He wouldn't move a muscle during the hitching process, but the second the motor started, he'd set his huge feet in the mud and lunge forward. Everything received a good splashing with muddy water, but the car invariably moved! Then, while the grateful driver was offering to pay for his services, Barney was released and he'd trot peacefully back to the barn to await another summons.

In the 1940s we still put up hay with a loader in the field and a hay fork in the barn. Barney provided the power on the hay rope, and soon learned to pull forkfuls of hay up into the barn all by himself—no driver was needed. At the command "Go, Barney!" he'd walk briskly down the barnhill, pulling up the load until he felt the rope slacken as the weight hit the track. Then he'd turn and come back up and station himself near the barn, ready for the next trip.

He did this job perfectly for many summers with but one accident. Late one June afternoon all of us, including Barney, were hot and tired while finishing our last load of the day. As Barney was part way down the hill with his load, the neighbor's big dog came from nowhere and barked loudly at his heels. The startled horse veered in a sharp half-circle to the left, and the taut hay rope came around and upset the weathered little outhouse completely off its old stone foundation! If a horse can look humiliated, Barney certainly did that time.

One spring day Barney had to pull harder than ever before. My husband had taken the old pickup with a load of fertilizer to a field to plant corn, and it had dropped through a dry crust into a wet spot and was tightly stuck. When he came to the kitchen door with Barney, I knew something was wrong.

"I'm stuck. Will you come and lead Barney while I drive the pickup? It's in pretty deep, and I'm afraid he can't move it alone even if he thinks he can."

I followed them to the field and patted Barney's nose as he was being hitched. "Keep to the side," my husband warned. "When I start the motor he'll really pull—you know how he is."

At the first sound, the eager horse gave his usual powerful lunge, but the truck moved only a few inches. I pulled the rope and urged him on, and he gave another lunge. This time a hame strap broke, and Barney went forward nearly on his nose—so fast that I let go of the rope because I couldn't keep up.

And as I stood there and stared, the entire harness scattered out behind him—leaving the huge bare collar hanging lonely and ludicrous

around his neck. Knowing that something out of the ordinary had happened, Barney turned and looked inquisitively at the jumbled mess. His whole mien expressed such puzzlement that I was compelled to laugh, and after a minute my husband joined in.

Barney, ignoring what he must have considered our silly response to the matter, walked back, turned, and stationed himself in front of the pickup again, as though to say, "Well, come on—let's give it another try!"

Barney worked hard and willingly around the farm, surprising us many times with his "horse sense". But as the years passed, changes gradually occurred that decreased our needs for "horsepower". Better roads were constructed, we started doing more of our work with a tractor, and the hay was baled.

Although we found less work for him to do, Barney's intelligent brown eyes looked so expectant when his bridle was taken from the peg. He backed so eagerly from the stall when harnessed, we didn't have the heart to disappoint him. Frankly, sometimes we relegated tasks to him that we might have done quicker some other way.

During his lifetime Barney helped to break a dozen or so colts, and a more patient, understanding teacher could not have been found. He always walked along with a firm, guiding step, seeming to know that "as the twig is bent…"

One morning when we went to the barn, everything was too quiet. There was no joyful little whinny of welcome we always heard from Barney. No brown eyes full of love. In the days that followed, there was not only a vacant stall in the barn, but also a vacant spot in our lives— a spot that had been filled for so long by a noble horse that had come to be almost like "family" to us.

A Daughter All Her Life

My daughter and I talk of many things, for we have shared in the sun and shadows of life.
Yet sometimes, still, when I glance at her, I see the little girl with flaxen braids who climbed into my lap for just another bedtime story.
—Helena Stefanski of Lakewood, Colorado

Pulling Mints Was Our Winter Fun

By Ruth Moose of Albermarle, North Carolina

On a cold, mid-December night, when it was clear, sharp and frosty, my father whistled into the house with a bulky, brown-wrapped package under his arm. Robbie, my younger brother, and I knew the time had come. Tonight we'd make mints.

We hung over the table as Daddy un-

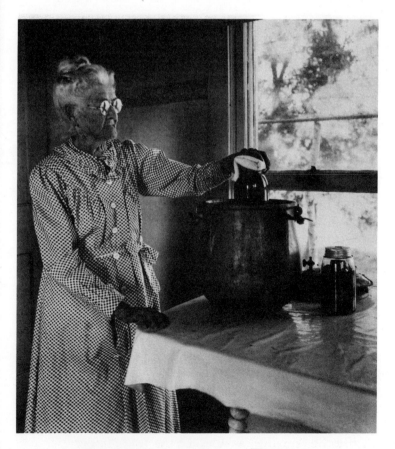

RURAL WOMEN *grew up learning how to can the bounty of the garden and, how to enjoy the sights, sounds and aromas of country living.*

wrapped for what seemed like forever. Finally fat bags of sugar rolled out, plus squares of *real* butter, a small drugstore bottle and glass dropper of real magic.

After supper, Mama hung up her apron and tucked a clean white dish towel around Daddy's waist. He held up his arms, turned on his toes as she fitted it, then left. We giggled as we rushed to get out the special pan, thermometer, wooden spoon, shears and waxed paper.

From the top shelf of our dark, floury-smelling pantry, we stood on stools to reach the tins. We wouldn't need them tonight, but we wanted to be ready. From its place beside the refrigerator, we tugged on the black-swirled marble slab. Daddy said it weighed a ton as he lifted it to the table.

I measured sugar, while Robbie lit the gas and then blew out the match. Daddy began to cut butter, his hand flat on the knife, and blocks of butter began falling like pale dominoes. These went atop the sugar, evenly sprinkled. Then water went over all. Last the thermometer was poked in, upright as a judge.

The pot bubbled. In the sugared air, we sang, happy as bees, watching and waiting.

When Daddy took the thermometer out and pronounced the creamy substance done, we stood back as he poured out a crystal puddle. We watched it spread...the edges rolled out, scalloped and thin, then stopped within our buttered space.

We leaned over the puddle, and Daddy, elbows out and the small bottle in his hands, let the genie from the glass dropper. Oil of peppermint. The smell of it was so strong I expected it to take a shape, ask our commands.

Next the milky edges of the candy were lifted, fluted all around like a huge pie shell as they cooled. We all buttered our twice-clean hands. Daddy stretched a hank of candy rope, looped it and brought it back again. "It's all in the wrist," he said, twisting, looping, snapping.

We tried. We really tried. The warm candy was heavy in our hands, like something alive and bent on escape. Daddy always took our rope back, stretched it around and over, slick and shiny. He pulled faster, harder.

Robbie and I stretched waxed paper atop the freezer, the washer, tray table, even the seat of an extra chair. Daddy patted the ribbed snake, then snipped it into bits. Rows of rectangular buttons appeared. The mints had to cream, Daddy said, and we went to bed sleepy-eyed and full of secrets.

Each day Robbie and I tested. Were they creamed yet? Still sticky, chewy as taffy. On the fourth day they were light as clouds, like winter ice and snow melting soft and cool down the backs of our throats, the taste lingering on our tongues. We put the mints into jars and tins, topped with pretty bows.

And we carried them like prizes to school. Merry Christmas to our teachers, the principal at the glass-topped desk, Willie in the furnace room, Velma and Bernice, starched white and bustling in the cafeteria. Nobody was supposed to buy gifts for teachers. It was a school rule. But nobody said you couldn't make things for gifts.

At lunch my teacher asked, "Did your mother make these?" as she held the half-emptied jar and smiled. "They're delicious."

"No ma'm," I said. "My father did. We helped."

"Of course," she said. "Tell your mother how much I liked them. How good they are."

"But she didn't..." I stopped. You never corrected a teacher. Later I heard Miss Martin in the hall, sharing her mints with the fifth-grade teacher next door. "Aren't these marvelous? Ruth's mother made them."

That night I told Daddy. He laughed. Robbie said his teacher said the same thing. Last year's teacher had, too. "Your mother." We laughed, reached our warm hands into the tin and shared the last of the leftover mints, the buttery crumbs and, best of all...a family secret.

Summer Was Fun At the Bendin' Tree

By Ruth Williamson Harden of Texarkana, Texas

Love's Pool was just below the chicken yard, over a three-strand wire fence and down a steeply slanting hill where pure white dogwood bloomed in early spring. It wasn't called by that name because of any amorous goings on there, but because a family named Love owned the farm joining ours, where this small body of water was located.

Green willows trailed their graceful branches along its edges and its waters were filled with small perch and snakes native to east Texas. On warm days we fished there, keeping our eyes peeled for little crawling creatures. After supper, as the stars came out over the sycamores, we sat on the porch and listened to the frogs raising their voices in jubilation.

Just to the left of the levee stood our bendin' tree, a big old sweet gum which stood proud and straight until my sister's 12th birthday party. That day, having exhausted all the games the adults planned for the occasion, we looked about for livelier diversions. We wandered into the pasture and idly threw stones into the pool until two of the larger boys, noticing the young tree, pulled it to the ground and placed several of us astride its trunk. They let it up as far as their arms would reach, then down again. We took turns for this exhilarating ride, standing in line like passengers for the subway. It was not only the hit of the party, but it became the favorite gathering spot all that summer for us and our cronies.

The tree remained permanently bent, but continued to grow, its branches shooting up to form other small trees. One of the tree's upper tips was so close to the ground the smallest of us could step into its leafy greenness and sit, half hidden by branches, while we read or fished or dreamed and the dragonflies touched down softly

31

on the sun-dappled water.

The bendin' tree was a haven of refuge the day my cousin and I sought shelter there after being chased across the pasture by an unfriendly bull. Clutching straw hats and dolls, we hung on for dear life until the enraged animal lost interest in his prey and trotted over the hill, his angry bellows echoing through the trees.

It was in that tree that we held a contest on a summer afternoon with the cousins, deciding who could faint the most realistically. We commenced swooning all over the hill, and my sister, who always had a flair for the dramatic, fell slowly to the ground, throwing her right hand gracefully behind her and wrist deep into a fresh cow pile. Rising with her dignity intact, she stalked toward the house, her very back registering disgust, while we fell all over each other and howled with laughter.

Years later I stood on what was once the levee and looked for familiar landmarks. There were none. The bendin' tree had vanished but other sweet gums had sprung up and they stood tall and straight, as it once had.

Perhaps it was their leaves rustling in the wind, but for one moment I was sure I heard the murmur of remembered voices and the faint sound of childish laughter.

To Grandma, They Were "Receipts"

By Charlotte Lanham of Danbury, Wisconsin

Grandma's receipt drawer in the cabinet was the small one almost overlooked between the flour bin and the sugar container. It wasn't until I was in sixth-grade cooking class and our teacher spoke about recipes that I knew they were ever called anything else but receipts.

"Now, girls," she said, "I am hearing some of you saying receipts. Your mothers probably used this word, but from now on I want you to call them recipes. A receipt is a written statement given for a paid bill or amount of goods," she concluded.

When I repeated teacher's words to Grandma, she said that was just a lot of highfalutin' nonsense! All those bits of paper in the little drawer were her receipts!

"I keep a lot of them in my head, too," she went on. "For instance, I didn't need a receipt for Tiny Broughton's sweet-sour beans. I could tell about what was in it without askin', and, anyway, it isn't polite to ask a cook how she makes anything. Tell 'em if you like the dish. Then if they offer to give you the receipt, that's fine.

"If they don't, when you get home write down what you think was in it. After you make it a few times and you 'add to', you'll have your own receipt." Grandma had a sharp sense of taste, and this was easy for her to do.

I have wonderful memories of food and cooking from being raised by Grandma and Grandpa. Grandma could cook anything without measuring.

Whatever she made came out just right ...like her apple pies! Many times I watched as she put flour, lard and salt in a bowl and blended it to a crumbly stage with her fingers. After adding just enough water to make it all stick together, she rolled it out on a floured board and fit it into her pie tin, reserving the remainder for the top crust.

This she deftly folded in half, then cut with alternating rows of slits to let out steam as the pie baked. When the apples were added she put a little sugar over the top, and a bit of cinnamon, a pinch of salt and a shake or two from the nutmeg can, and dotted the whole inside with bits of butter.

Then, after dipping her finger in water, she slid it around the rim and placed the folded crust on top, holding the pie aloft while she trimmed the extra dough away with her paring knife.

After she crimped the edges together between thumb and forefinger, she went over to thrust her hand inside the oven of the wood stove to see if the temperature was just right.

When the pie crust was golden brown she brought it from the oven and deposited it on the tin-covered counter of the cabinet to cool. I could scarcely wait!

She told me when she was 12 she helped in the kitchen of a hotel in southern Illinois. One day the baker failed to come to work. Having watched the pies being made so long she offered to try doing them and did so well she was asked to continue making all the pies from then on. No wonder she was such an expert by the time I came along.

When I married I asked her how to make some of my favorites, this being a privilege reserved for family members. She guessed mostly but offered to write down what she did remember. I could leave off or add to, she said, until I came up with whatever tasted about right.

"You'll soon get the knack of it," she told me, but I never came anywhere near to the sweet rolls she called rusks. They were a yeast dough made of graham and white flour, butter, nutmeg, brown sugar and a bit of salt, and they stood tall in the pan as they came from the oven ready to have glaze drizzled over them.

When Grandma passed away and some of the furnishings were distributed among us, I looked through the receipt drawer first. There were many separate slips of paper there, all written in her curlicue kind of writing—some with a cryptic word or two written alongside in fading ink, as though that ingredient might have been an oversight and added as an afterthought.

Anyone who cooked could decipher the abbreviations used in the "receipt" for potato pancakes—"grate pot., flour, B.P., S. and P. Fry."

For molasses cookies, I read "Usual cookie dough. Sorghum. Use buttermilk and cold coffee." The secret of the softness of her cookies apparently was the sorghum, and the coffee addition gave that special flavor.

Frickadillies! Oh, how I enjoyed those cakes of leftover beef, potatoes and onions! The only directions said "Cut up beef, pot., onion, egg, salt. Fry." Then in small letters down at the bottom, "watch close. Burns easy." Did they ever!

For her potato soup Grandma added what she called "riffles". The paper read, "Egg, not too much flour, will be stiff. Roll, cut in strips, drop in soup a few at a time."

For Dip, a sauce she served over bread pudding or cake, one tattered paper said, "Make a paste, flour, sugar, salt, cold water. Add boiling water, cinnamon, nutmeg, butter. Boil smooth!" This one was written in more detail, as though she thought I might have trouble with it. I did, in spite of the details. It was a long time before I came up with a smooth Dip.

Late summer found Grandma making catsup, painstakingly filling rows of bottles with the aid of a funnel, corking them carefully, then dipping them in hot, red sealing wax to store in the cellar for our winter use.

I can still envision her standing there in the overheated kitchen, dipping her finger in cold water before she pushed the wax close

CALLIN' 'em "recipes" was just high-falutin' nonsense to Grandma. Her word for those treasured instructions was "receipts".

33

around the cork, then putting it over on the cabinet to cool along with the other bottles there. The Heinz people could have taken lessons from her.

There were the other kinds of receipts in the drawer as well—written statements for paid bills, receipts for tons of coal, for rent, for furniture and curtains bought "on time" and even for the Maytag washer which stood in the corner of the kitchen covered with an old oilcloth.

There were also receipts for rent on the half-double house on Arsenal where we paid $25 per month and had a basement furnace and a bathroom for the first time. We were all working then, and times were good.

Later, when things were tougher, we moved back to the old neighborhood and lived in another half-double house for $18 a month. Grandpa was too old to work then, and our income was less.

The receipt drawer was, in truth, a journal of our lives, recording as it did the rising cost of coal and rent. There was never a more true picture of our day-to-day living or how it had changed through the years.

I kept all those bits of paper from the receipt drawer for a long time. Then one rainy day at housecleaning time, while thumbing through them once more, I came across the directions for making a Bob Andy pie! Robert Andrew somebody-or-other's favorite dessert. How could I have missed it before?

But there it was, directions for making that delicate spicy custard confection from southern Indiana! Once tasted it was seldom forgotten. It took several attempts before I came up with a perfect pie. However, it was well worth the effort.

My cooking teacher wouldn't be particularly pleased to know I didn't stop saying receipts, especially when I spoke of those from the little cabinet drawer. Whichever they are, I use them often and cherish them very much. One day they will be passed along for the enjoyment of others, and Grandma's receipts will live again in other places and other times.

Those Old-Time Ailments Had Nasty Cures!

By Sara Brandon of Phoenix, Arizona

That old adage "The cure is worse than the ailment" certainly held true for us children who grew up 40 years ago. The things we were forced to ingest, inhale, or get rubbed on, were incredible! But, some of them must have worked, or else I wouldn't be here to tell this intriguing story.

Take colds, for instance. When I was a child, the first step in curing a cold was to "clean out the system". This was done by downing castor oil in orange juice, or by drinking a half-bottle of citrate of magnesia. (Usually we held our noses.)

Chest congestion treatments were a bit more complicated. Our skinny rib cages were rubbed with camphorated oil, or musterole, then hot flannel cloths (which Mama heated in the oven) were applied to our chests. In more stubborn cases, she used a mustard plaster on us, which was supposed to draw out the infection.

Oh the pain and screams when the time came for removing those mustard plasters! More often than not, some of our skin came up along with them.

We dreaded sore throats even more. When we saw our mother squeezing lemons, we hoarsely screamed that our throats didn't hurt at all anymore. But this didn't daunt her. She added salt to the lemon juice, carefully wrapped her right index finger with a piece of silk cloth, dipped her finger into the juice, then proceeded to swab out throats, while we gagged and struggled under her grasp.

Finally, she put an old flannel cloth around our necks to keep the cold out.

My husband says his grandmother was even a bit meaner than my mother. Every spring he had to take one tablespoon of kerosene with sugar to "clean out his system". His grandmother used flaxseed poultices for infections.

My grandmother loved to get into the act and often tried to doctor us in her best "Mammy Yokum" manner.

If she decided our eyes looked glassy, and we rubbed our noses too often, it was a sure indication that we had worms. The treatment for this was to rub garlic around the eyes, nose and navel! The intestinal worms, if we had them, surely vanished, because even they couldn't stand that smell for very long!

Infections or boils were treated less dramatically. Grandmother burned a cloth until it was reduced to ashes, mixed the ashes with olive oil, then rubbed the concoction onto the infected area, binding the sore with a soft cloth.

My mother's favorite remedy for infections was hot bread and milk poultices. But the bread and milk might have been put to better use helping cure our tummy aches, instead of her bay leaf tea, which was the customary remedy.

To relieve an earache, my sister-in-law remembers that her father made a very tight funnel out of paper and inserted the small end into the child's ear. Then the paper was set afire and the smoke blown into the patient's ear.

Her dad claimed the smoke would cure the ache. I'm sure a pan of water was kept handy, in case the child's hair caught fire in the process of treatment. The cure, I have no doubt, resulted more from fear, than from the smoke!

All this reminiscing has given me a headache, so I think I'll go bind my head with a headache band, just as my mother used to do for me when I suffered head pains. Maybe as an extra precaution, I'll take a couple of aspirin, too, just to be on the safe side!

Yesterday's Cures Were Just Unbelievable!

By Lee Duncan of Lexington, Kentucky

Our ancestors bottled their home remedies, so it wasn't necessary to slap on a dozen labels with as many "cautions" as we find on today's health aids.

My father had a cough potion, handed down from one generation to another, and I still use it in preference to a powerful drug that will reduce me to a state of apathy for weeks—he prepared a simple mixture of rock candy, honey and whiskey.

As a child, I was afraid to cough after a slug of that potion because I thought the whiskey would explode through my throat in a great ball of fire. I got this idea from listening to an evangelist who preached hell fire and damnation to those who tipped the bottle.

Yesterday's cure for poison oak or ivy was rather drastic—"wash with 2 teaspoons of soda to a pint of water and wet cloths applied with extract of hamammellis."

If you don't know what hamammellis is, don't worry about it—the next part of the treatment would eliminate all the poison in your system, anyway—"After covering affected parts, take a dose of Epsom salts."

I'm partial to remedies using spirits other than "spirits of turpentine" and one for fever and ague is my favorite: "4 ounces galangal root in a quart of gin to be taken often."

Since folks used spirits in many remedies, they also had a cure for drunkards—"pulverize one pound of fresh, quill-red Peruvian bark and soak in one pint of diluted alcohol, strain and evaporate down to one half pint. For two days, take a tablespoon every 3 hours, on the third day one half teaspoon, on the fourth reduce to 15 drops, then to 10, then to 5. Seven days will cure the dastardly drunkard."

On occasion, our grandmothers got technical as to proportions for a remedy. To eliminate tapeworms, they advised, "omit supper and breakfast, then the next morning take one-third part of 200 minced pumpkin seeds, remove shells with hot water before taking dose. At nine of the clock take another third, at 10 the remainder. Follow at 11 with a strong dose of castor oil."

Most remedies were reasonable and fairly effective, but there is one that even my Victorian mind cannot comprehend—probably because I haven't had an opportunity to test it on anyone! It advised "to restore a patient struck by lightning, shower with cold water for 2 hours. If patient does not show signs of life, put salt in the water and continue to shower an hour longer."

Some of the old-fashioned beauty aids were slightly drastic. For extra hairs on the face, the word was "best left alone". But some couldn't resist a favorite remedy—"spread on a piece of leather, equal parts of garbanum and pitch plaster, lay on hair for 3-4 minutes. This is severe but it will remove hair, root and branch." I

figure this one needed a caution label advising "may remove the face."

For a harmless complexion wash, our grandmothers used one ounce of powdered gum of benzoin in a pint of whiskey placed in a container of water until it turned milky. To clear a tanned skin they used a solution of carbonate of soda, lemon juice and the juice of unripe grapes.

If you wanted to go all the way and remove those hateful wrinkles you could use an ounce of white wax, 2 ounces of strained honey and 2 ounces of the juice of lily-bulbs melted and stirred together. To clean out the pores, a few drops of ammonia in water took the place of soap! Wow!

For a beautiful complexion, ladies used tar or oatmeal soap and glycerine. However one caution was added—"if this method is used, it would be just as well to keep the knowledge of it from the gentlemen."

One beautiful lady who had not washed her face for 3 years had a clean, rosy, sweet skin, but she made the mistake of telling her sweetheart about her beauty secret.

The ending is sad, but her beau said, "I cannot reconcile my heart and my manhood to a woman who hasn't washed her face for 3 years."

Ladies, you may share the remedies, but keep your beauty secrets to yourself!

Threshing Day Made Summer Complete

By Madolyn Brown of Fall River, Wisconsin

The look of summer's golden fields stirring under the hot breath of August always fills me with threshing-day memories. Today's harvesttime assault by huge combines which ravage a sea of grain and reduce it to scattered blocks of gold will never create anything to equal them...

Thirty-seven years ago, threshing day was a high spot in the summer of a farm child—com-

parable in excitement to the last day of school and far more thrilling than the Fourth of July.

Each person's memories come from his or her vantage point or particular interest. While my brother might today reminisce about the size of a straw stack one special summer or teams of horses stomping their feet and chewing his hand-fed grass, it is the kitchen that I remember best of all.

On threshing day, the kitchen seemed to be the busiest place on the farm, rustling with activity before the men were out of bed to milk and still in operation long after darkness had shut down the fieldwork.

Threshing day was not a day for a child to lie abed and listen to the roosters crow. There was far too much to do. But no matter how early I stumbled downstairs, it was always too late to find the cool, relatively quiet kitchen of any other morning. Half a dozen different jobs were already under way.

Even at this early hour there were pies baking in the oven and others cooling on the windowsill and table in the pantry, their aromas mingling in a mouth-watering scent.

Soon the kitchen began to fill. One or two ladies always arrived early with their husbands and immediately pitched in to help. Other neighbors would appear, bustling and red-faced, closer to noon to assist with the "dishing up". Each entered the kitchen carrying a contribution to the meal. Specialties had to be tasted and praised in a ritual that never varied...Mrs. Johnson's baked beans, Grandma Myer's potato salad, Mrs. Ryan's chocolate layer cake.

There was an almost partylike atmosphere in the kitchen, and if a youngster stayed out of the way and kept busy carrying water and wood or swatting flies, it was possible to be a part of it all.

As noon approached, the women worked at a faster pace. Now the chatter subsided and quiet prevailed as bread was sliced, potatoes mashed, pies cut, gravy stirred, glasses filled and meat carved. These last-minute preparations had all the timing of the final moments before a rocket launch.

The sounds of the men, laughing and joking as they washed the morning's evidence of hard work from their faces and arms, made the women step even faster. They scurried around the kitchen like ants at an anthill, but at the stroke of 12, everything came together in a display of precision that would have made any moon launch seem disorganized by comparison.

The men entered the house and sat around the table in almost identical bib overalls and worn, blue-cambric shirts—they had the look of uniforms. Each face was tanned to the middle of the forehead, then stark white to the hairline.

When the last chair had scraped into place, the door from the kitchen opened and the ladies entered, proudly bearing bowls, platters and pitchers.

There was roast beef or pork and baked ham, mashed potatoes and gravy, cabbage salad, cucumber and tomato salad, baked beans,

scalloped corn, fresh rolls and pies, hot coffee, cold lemonade and garden relishes of every variety. It was enough to make anybody's eyes water with desire.

Threshing etiquette provided that the children eat last, and each year there was much apprehension as we watched mounds of food disappear with no letup in the fork-to-mouth motion of the men. It seemed as though they would never get filled up. I remember standing on tiptoe, peeking into the dining room window from the front yard, where we had been exiled, marveling at the crew's eating capacity.

We need not have worried about going hungry, though, for there was always more food in the kitchen, and empty bowls were quickly replenished. It was a point of honor to never run out of food for the ravenous men. Only young brides ever suffered this embarrassment—but never more than once.

"Any beans left, Ev?"

"Could I have a bit more raspberry pie, Miz Millson?"

At last—the last bit of gravy was swabbed off a plate by a crust of bread and the last drop of coffee was drained from a cup. Again chairs scraped, and contented conversion began as the men went outside to lie under the trees and talk while their dinner settled. They had eaten in almost total silence.

Now it was our turn. The women began to reset the main table for their own meal, but first the youngsters were graciously allowed to grab a plate and help themselves in a casual buffet manner.

We thought the ladies most kind to let us forget our manners and grab and run, but years later, I realized our mothers only wanted a little peace and quiet and a second cup of coffee before they began to clean up the dishes and reset the table for the evening supper.

Our noon meal was consumed outside under the trees, within a respectful listening distance of the men. This truly was an era when the adage "Children should be seen but not heard" applied.

After seconds, thirds and sometimes fourths, we lay in discomfort, stomachs tight, under the huge elm trees on the front lawn, soothed by the hot, dry breezes of summer.

For me, everything after dinner was anticlimactic. With us too full for comfort, there was no time to run off the meal. The kitchen now held mountains of dishes awaiting attention.

My job of drying dishes seemed interminable. I would hang up each soaking flour-sack towel and reach for a dry one in an almost automatic manner, while tiny trails of sweat ran down my back. The shiny faces of the women were outlined with wisps of wet hair. Hairdos loosened and gave up.

I'll never marry a farmer, I vowed, as I stood in that suffocating room. My young imagination couldn't visualize combines and microwave ovens, water heaters, dishwaters and air conditioners—magic to make life easier. At 10, I thought things would never change.

I would stay out from underfoot and listen to the woman talk of recipes and everyday matters, straining to hear when voices were lowered, knowing that something deliciously adult was being discussed.

I always partook less heartily of the evening meal, for by then I was too tired to care about food. After picking at the still-abundant

offerings—cold sliced meat, accompanied by home-baked bread to sandwich it, potato salad, vegetable salads, pickled peaches and apple rings, plus cake and freshly cranked ice cream for dessert—I would sneak off to my room before anyone could draft me into another job.

I lay on my bed in the stuffy room above the kitchen, lulled by the murmur of voices from below and the muffled sound of rattling dishes and slamming cupboard doors, with never a pang of conscience. At this self-centered stage of my life, it didn't enter my head to wonder if the women were tired, if their backs ached or their feet hurt.

Today, in the comfort of my own modern kitchen outfitted with its many appliances, I think back to those times and marvel at how the women managed.

The day was long and the work was hard, but no one complained, for it was threshing day. And on threshing day everyone gave a little extra to get the job done.

Mysterious Gift Meant So Much to Her

By Kathy Gray of Tacoma, Washington

Believe it or not, I was pushing 30 before I owned my own Foley. Aunt Nora couldn't rest easy until I had one.

My aunt used to say to my uncle, "Art, we've got to buy Kathy a Foley."

Well, I didn't know what one was, either. But I didn't dare play dumb in front of them. In fact I was embarrassed to ask anyone about it. The word wasn't even in the dictionary. So I silently nodded and smiled whenever she brought up the subject.

When Aunt Nora first mentioned it I was about 25 and I rather hoped that I wouldn't die without possessing a Foley. But she was not the type to be pushed. I knew her pretty well, as I had spent many weekends with the two of them

on the farm when I was growing up. In my middle 20's I still spent time with Aunt Nora and Uncle Art, and my husband was very fond of them, too.

When Uncle Art took the 4-mile trip to town in his old pickup for groceries, he always managed to get a few extra cans of soup or loaves of bread or a box of detergent and bring it over to our house. When our kids saw him drive up they scrambled to see what he'd brought.

On many of those occasions I'd expectantly look out the window, and, in addition to the store items, I'd spy homegrown radishes, onions and things. Each time Uncle Art visited I hoped he'd say, "Well Kathy, here's your Foley at last. Keep it in good health."

There I was, a grown woman with kindergarten, mud puddles, a dirty bathtub—and a Foley on my mind. I just knew if Aunt Nora died without buying it for her favorite niece, I'd never have the privilege of touching one.

I was certain they could afford such a luxury, but remembered my aunt was quite a procrastinator. Since she was more or less the boss in their marriage, she took a year or so to make up her mind about a new housedress, a vacuum cleaner or ceramic bird.

Knowing this, I was patient with my aunt in her later years. Even when we talked frequently on the phone I didn't bug her about the Foley. After all, it was her money.

Then one fall day Uncle Art and Aunt Nora pulled into our driveway in the pickup. The back was full of various kinds of fresh apples from their orchard. I knew I'd be busy making cobbler for a while. But I didn't know there was a brown paper bag in the cab of the truck just for me—containing a brand new Foley.

After we exchanged greetings, Aunt Nora reached for the sack and handed it to me with pleasure. "Well, I told Art to buy you your Foley today. Here it is."

Like a kid inside but a 30-year-old outside, I slowly separated the staples from the top of the bag, reached in with my right hand, and came up with a shiny, stainless-steel food mill for making applesauce. On the handle in huge letters, the brand name FOLEY stuck out, and I guess my face looked sort of funny.

Applesauce, indeed—who would have ever thought!

"Thanks." I said it, not believing what had happened. Then I saw in my mind a replica of my shiny Foley hanging on Aunt Nora's kitchen wall and almost tasted the hot applesauce with cinnamon she'd made for so many years. My eyes sparkled a little as I realized it was important to her that I have this gift. The recollection hit me—she addressed all refrigerators as Frigidaires and to her, every washer in the world was a Maytag. I should have known a Foley was an applesauce maker.

I did teach my children how to make applesauce from Aunt Nora's recipe. Even the youngest got the hang of turning the handle round and round until everything but the peelings and core sieved through the Foley.

The thrill of being first to taste your own homemade applesauce is a memory no one can take away.

WOULDN'T this woman from years back have loved her very own Foley for apple season? Homemade applesauce is the best!

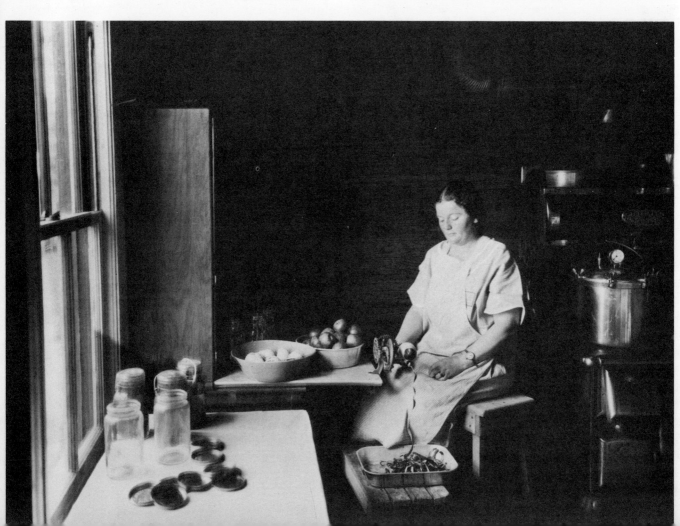

Thank Goodness For Toasty Featherbeds!

By Zoe Rexroad of Adrian, Missouri

My feet get cold even now when I think of that long trip from the cozy dressing spot behind the Round Oak heating stove to the bedroom upstairs! When I was a kid, that seemed like The Last Mile.

Although I never voiced an opinion, I often wondered why Mother and Dad got to sleep in a warm bedroom downstairs, while all four of us children had to climb to dreaded chilly heights and enter an icy-cold bedroom.

Just as they do today, admonitions to get ready for bed drew vigorous protests. But unlike children of today, who protest because they don't want to leave their cherished spot in front of TV, our objections came because of the blast we would receive when we opened the door to go upstairs.

Bare steps and bare floors greeted bare feet, and by the time we had made our way to the bed, threw back the covers and climbed in, we were shaking from head to foot.

But this was the point in time when the one redeeming feature of our beds was welcomed and appreciated—the fabulous featherbed!

Although I didn't realize it at the time, Mother braved that cold domain every day to plump up those feathers, so we'd be able to sink down into that downy softness at night.

Making four featherbeds required as much energy as a modern-day jogger would expend on a 5-mile jaunt! Those feathers had to be fluffed up every morning—for after sleeping on them, they were mashed flat as the proverbial pancake. Feathers do not spring back on their own. They needed Mother's touch.

She would stand on one side of the bed, grab the edges of the ticking and start shaking like an angry dog killing a rattlesnake...this forced the feathers to the opposite side of the bed. The feathers piled up in a huge, fluffy mound. Then Mother would pull the ticking toward her and flip the featherbed over.

When it was turned, she pushed and smoothed the feathers until they were the same depth all over the bed. Sometimes she would run the handle of a broom over the featherbed to make it smooth. Putting on the sheets and beautiful hand-pieced quilts required special patience, for everywhere the bed was touched an indentation remained.

Where all those feathers came from to fill the ticking, I do not know, for we didn't keep ducks or geese. But I do know many farm women kept fowl in those days, mainly for their feathers. Ducks could be plucked throughout the summer —usually every 6 weeks—and the feathers were saved until enough accumulated to make a feather pillow or a featherbed.

Sometimes duck feathers were sold for a dollar a pound, and it takes a heck of a lot of duck feathers to make a pound! I suspect Mother bought our featherbeds already made.

Sometimes on an extra-cold night, we would find that Mother had slipped a heated flatiron wrapped in flannel cloth under the covers of our bed. It was literally heaven to feel the warmth of that iron against our feet!

Underneath each featherbed was a mattress of some kind. In summer we didn't want the featherbed plumped up, for it curled up around you and made scorching nights even worse.

Airing the featherbeds was done four or five times a year, when weather permitted. Mother and one of the older children would drag those featherbeds down the stairs and throw them over the propped-up clothesline for a day in the sun.

Slipping into a bed of freshly aired feathers and line-dried sheets was a privilege never forgotten. The sweet smell of country air lulled us to sleep and pleasant dreams. I keenly remember those nights even as I write. But then, I guess everything gets better and better in retrospect.

Although I don't own a waterbed, when I see an advertisement for one, I think to myself that it probably *would* beat the old featherbed. It is soft. It springs back after a touch. Its automatic heat control beats a heated iron all to holler.

I look at our beds, and I think that even they, with their extra firm innerspring mattresses and electric blankets, beat featherbeds by a good mile. (I can turn off the electric blanket, straighten the sheets, pull up the blanket and bedspread in 2 minutes flat, if I'm in a hurry!)

But when I was a kid, fabulous featherbeds were wonderful.

Autograph Book Brings Back Memories

By Margaret Buell Allen of Pasadena, California

Right there in the center of the bottom drawer was a little book. I was sorting out Grandmother's things a while back and there it was.

A bunch of red and white flowers were painted on the cover beneath the dingy, gilded word "Autographs". The pages were yellow, with loose and broken stitching in the binding, and the edges were worn.

The inscriptions were faded and accidental smudges were often camouflaged with drawings of lopsided flowers. Surely that little book had known life's stress and strain, as have many of us.

The book is dated 1881. To me, it evokes a picture of grandmother, little Lizzie, in a dress of plaid wool and a white pinafore to keep it clean. Her black wool stockings probably itched except where her long winter underwear covered her legs. She probably wore high button shoes and her hair in braided loops with plaid hair bows.

Maybe the autograph book was a birthday gift, I thought, passed around at school for the inscriptions of eager friends.

Most of the offerings are dripping with sentiment—naturally—like one signed by Etta:
"My love to you I can unfold,
'Tis like the ring that's made of gold,
'Tis fine, 'tis round and has no end,
So is my love for you, my friend."
In Grandmother's autograph book, friendship is the noble underlying theme. For example

one morale booster came from Maggie:
"When this you see, remember me
And bear me in your mind.
And I will be a friend to you
When others are unkind."
Most of the verses were addressed "To my friend and schoolmate". Angie wrote:
"Rember me early, rember me late,
And never forget your old schoolmate."
(Fourth-graders can't spell either, Angie.)

As a friendship symbol, the forget-me-not verse was a natural. Written all neat and proper was this note to my grandmother:
Friend Lizzie,
"There is a little flower that grows in
yonder cot,
It whispers all I wish to say, that is—
'forget me not'."
Your friend and schoolmate,
Willie Batchelder, January 11th, 1881
On another page little Nettie wrote:
'Tis sweet to be remembered,
'Tis sad to be forgot,
As in this world I wander,
Dear friend, forget me not."
Maudie's autograph book message was an easy one:
"Forget me not. Forget me never,
'Till the rising sun goes down forever."
Religious sentiments were popular autograph book verses and even more impressive than other types. One yellowed page had Minnie's contribution:
"To you may life be sweet,
Its pathway strewn with flowers.
May angels garde you safe

To the shade of edon's bowers."
(Minnie, you and Angie have the same problem, but poor spelling can't interfere with noble character.)

Edith sounds like she may have grown up to become a Sunday school teacher, but her penmanship would not have qualified:

"She know the Good Shephers Guards
His flock by day and night,
And the lambs are folded safely in the
Dark as in the light."

The following reminder of earth's temporal joys, written by Tillie, was typical of Grandmother's day:

"Remember, oh remember,
As the carefree moments fly,
The youngest one among us
Is not too young to die."

The verses were seldom original, but were plagiarized from one autograph book to another. The most popular autographer had the best instant recall of popular verses!

We have become less sentimental since those days. But to the young of the 1800s the book was a symbol of fond devotion for "dear schoolmates".

Saturday Night Meant Well-Earned Fun!

By Elaine Derendinger of Franklin, Missouri

Our small town made a mistake, I think, when stores switched from staying open late on Saturday to late hours on Friday!

Saturday night in town was always a special thing when I was growing up—and Friday night has never had that certain special charm.

Back then a farmer quit work a bit early on Saturday afternoon. Usually the hired man (at least in our area) took off at noon on Saturday. We kids didn't have to be reminded to get the chores done. (The cow may have wondered why she was being rushed to the barn to be milked when the sun was still high in the sky and the grass tasted so good.)

Daddy loaded a case of eggs and a can of cream in the car trunk and off we went.

I don't know why, but the men in the family always rode in the front. The women (Mother, my sister and I) sat in back.

Daddy didn't drive fast but we always had trouble with the windows. The men wanted them down, to enjoy the summer breeze, and we wanted them up so our hair wouldn't blow out of place!

If the sun was bright, Mother pinned a newspaper over her window to keep it out.

We always hoped to get to town in time for a good parking place. "Good" meant right on Main Street, preferably in the block between the dime store and J.C. Penney's, because everybody who was in town would doubtless walk down this block during the evening.

The main reason for the trip—and there had to be one—was to do the trading at the grocery—our eggs and cream in exchange for the sugar, flour and provisions needed.

I also remember taking eggs and cream to the feed store, where we picked up chicken feed in big sacks. We women always picked the bags—after all, we would end up wearing them or looking at them somewhere in the house eventually.

Those tasks done, the men would go off up the street and we would drop in on a store or two. The dime store was great for small things like envelopes or a can of talcum.

I was usually given a nickel to spend. You could use 5¢ in lots of ways then—a coloring book, small toy or candy bar! (Such a big decision!)

Mother usually went in the dry goods store and got thread and maybe a length of cotton. We usually walked in back to see if the new fall hats had come in.

Out on the street, we often walked down one block to look in the windows of the shoe store and ladies' ready-to-wear clothes. We seldom bought anything but it was fun to look.

Then it was back to the car to "watch the people". Sometimes a neighbor lady we knew would sit with us awhile and talk. The men stood around on the street or leaned against the buildings to talk. But women almost always sat in the car.

If I saw someone my own age that I knew we would venture up and down the street, giggling and whispering hand in hand. Small boys would do the same, but they walked much faster —and not hand in hand.

If a haircut was needed, Saturday night was the time to get it done so it was fresh for Sunday morning. I thought it was such fun to walk by the barbershop and look in and see the boys sitting there with a white cloth draped over them to catch the hair. They always looked so embarrassed!

Some women got their hair bobbed by the barber, but never on Saturday night—that belonged to the men. Once in a while, I went in with my mother. But I never really felt like I belonged there.

The men standing on the street talked about crops, livestock, the weather, farm sales coming up and how the new hired man was working out. In the car the women talked gardens, chickens, weather, who was expecting and who wasn't, illness, what a good-looking couple the newlyweds were—and look, there they are walking down the street now!

Sometimes older boys (who were extremely shy) would get up enough nerve on Saturday night to stop a certain girl on the street and ask if he could see her home. She, of course, had to ask her folks. Usually they said "yes" if she promised to be home early. And a new romance began.

Folks on the street began to thin out around 8:30. Stores stayed open until 9 p.m. There was no daylight saving time, just early-to-bed and early-to-rise. I suppose it did keep us healthy, wealthy and wise!

Often, just before we went home, we had a sack of candy from the dime store (a nice size bag for 5 or 10¢) or if it was a real hot, humid night, we could have an ice cream cone from the shop on the corner.

Then it was homeward bound. By the time we got there, I was usually half asleep. Tomorrow was Sunday with school and church— and then I could start looking forward to another wonderful Saturday night in town...our favorite time of the week!

Grandma's Cooking Heritage Rested at Noodle Table

By Linda Inman of Martinsville, Illinois

Grandma's noodle table doesn't belong anywhere anymore. It's in the garage, the yellow paint smudged, the white tin top faded, the four legs wobbling and looking completely out of place.

For years the 24-by-30-in. table was a part of Grandma's cluttered kitchen. It sat beside the cabinet with the tin doors and flour bin so that supplies for noodle making were within easy reach.

Formica countertops and built-in cabinets had no place in Grandma's kitchen. To her, efficiency planning meant you could use either gas or wood to cook with, depending on how hot the weather. Space was needed between the stove and the cabinets so the ashes could be cleaned easier, clothes could hang to dry and baby pigs could be warmed before taking them back to the barn.

A lot of pastries were mixed on the old tin top, but vivid in my memory are the noodles Grandma made while chicken pieces simmered on the stove.

Grandma never messed with dry noodles. She preferred to mix hers up while the chicken broth boiled. She would blend the eggs and salt and then begin adding flour and water, dusting the tin top with flour as the dough thickened. Grandma would mix and measure between trips to the stove to check on Sunday dinner.

Sunday dinner at Grandma's never varied much. The pies might be peach one time and apple the next, but the mainstay was always ham, noodles and mashed potatoes with various salads and vegetables.

Her noodles were always cooked in chicken broth, but then the chicken was boned and placed on its own plate because someone might not like them cooked together, and Grandma wouldn't offend anyone.

As the dough thickened, Grandma turned it out on the tin top and started rolling it gently, pushing it from the middle, out in all directions. Her fingers were deft and careful not to push too hard.

It was fun to watch Grandma mix and shape the dough, but cutting it was my favorite part. She had the handiest little gadget that she would slide through the dough and presto she had noodles. Light, tender noodles that didn't stick together or swell out of proportion.

I often think, as I pass the old table, how feeble my attempts at noodle making are compared to Grandma's. Mine gum together like yellow glue and what looks to me to be well-sized noodles, turn out the size of skinny boot strings even before they finish cooking.

Her table looks completely out of place next to our paneled garage walls, but maybe that's the best place for it after all. Looking at that table brings back memories of Grandma faster than thumbing through the family album does.

Grandma's Noodles

2 cups flour
1/2 teaspoon baking powder
1-1/2 to 2 teaspoons salt
3 whole eggs
1/2 an eggshell of either oil or cream (About 3
    teaspoons.) (Grandma used whichever she had.)

Mix flour, baking powder and salt in a bowl. Make a hollow place in the middle, add eggs and either cream or oil. With a fork or hands, gradually mix eggs and flour mixture until thickened. Turn out on floured board, knead gently for a few minutes. Roll dough thin, an 1/8th of an inch or less. Cut noodles and drop into boiling broth. Cook 15 minutes or until tender. (Makes about 1-1/2 pounds dry noodles or 12 cups cooked.)

Nobody Missed Out On Sunday's Family Dinner

By Helen Rawlings of Waterloo, Iowa

Along the road to modernism, one of the things that has slipped into oblivion is the family dinner every Sunday. At our house it was always at the middle of the day, and all members of the family were expected to be present. It was a traditional time to include relatives and friends.

If there were too many to seat comfortably in the dining room, a table in the kitchen provided seating for the small fry. That group was always within earshot of the adults' conversation and the kids had an ample view of the adults so everyone could determine who was getting older, hard of hearing, or just fat!

Sunday dinner was generally a jolly time and the laughter was infectious. If you didn't understand what the merriment was about, you laughed, too, because you just felt good inside when everyone else was that happy to be together. It was a time to catch up on all the news.

It was a time for special culinary treats. Everyone but Mother exerted themselves the least on that day, yet ate the most. Every hostess was noted for some specialty and you always hoped she'd serve that particular thing when you were invited to her house.

Often there were several desserts. My father's favorite was pie...mine, too. Dad would ask my mother, "What kind of pie do we have today?" When she'd reply "apple", "cherry", or whatever she'd made, he'd say, "Fine, then I'll have apple!" or whatever it was she'd told him.

The only bad thing about our special Sunday dinner was you had to wear your Sunday best and stay dressed up all day. It was a little more difficult to have a good time after dinner in good clothes. And you committed a mortal sin if you tore or stained something! Knees fell out of long white stockings so very easily, and an accident could cloud the remainder of the day for you.

After dinner the men clustered together to discuss politics, or the various businesses they were engaged in. If weather permitted, they gathered on the lawn to play catch, pass a football or pitch horseshoes.

Putting the food away and doing the dishes occupied the ladies, and simple preparations for supper sandwiches, coffee and fruit were finished so everyone could stay through the evening.

The women always exchanged patterns for sewing, crocheting or quilts and made arrangements to meet again and help each other with these projects.

Yes, those were the days—a real observance of Sunday and the Sabbath. It was a long-standing tradition. Whatever became of it?

For one thing, the advent of the automobile put people on wheels. They began using Sundays to go to places of entertainment, rather than stay home. Stores and shopping areas stayed open on Sunday to lure the wanderers.

Out of it all, mothers gained. They were freed from the kitchen on weekends, but I think society has paid a terrible price. Wouldn't it be wonderful if we could proclaim one Sunday a year as Family Dinner Sunday? It would be marvelous to see the art of conversation revived, with family members taking special time to get reacquainted.

BEFORE the age of television and modern entertainment, folks used to gather for all sorts of things...sharing ideas and swapping news!

3

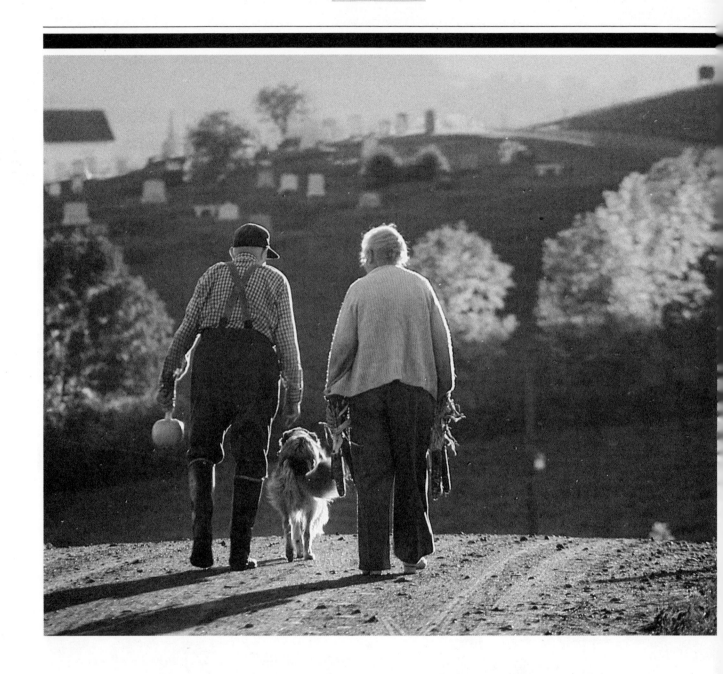

Blest Be the Tie That Binds
Country Neighbors, Country Kin

Chickens Taught About Love and Caring

By Marjorie Burris of Mayer, Arizona

They were a wedding gift, those first chickens, and they were everything a wedding gift is meant to be—something to help the young folks "get started". But they didn't just help us get started in material things. Those chickens taught us about love and caring and joy in the simple things of everyday life.

My husband was a young minister in a lively rural church when we got married. Even though I was a city girl, the congregation had aided and abetted our courtship. Somehow they knew I loved their farm ways and they were as eager to help me feel at home on the farm as I was to become one of them.

Soon after we were married, two women from the church came to see us.

"We wanted to give you something special for a wedding gift," one began hesitantly, as she looked at the other who was nodding encouragement. "Would you be offended if we brought you some layers?"

"Offended?" I echoed. "I'd be delighted!" What could make me feel more like a farm wife than having my own flock of chickens? I hugged both women.

My husband and I quickly got a little chicken house ready, and a couple of evenings later the women delivered the chickens. One woman brought seven Rhode Island Reds. The other gave us seven white leghorns. They were beautiful.

But when we put the hens in the house together for the first time, they took one look at each other and began to fight! Such squawking and pecking! Straw and feathers flew everywhere. At first the white chickens climbed on the roosts; then the red chickens edged them off.

Not satisfied to sleep on the floor, the white birds started flying back on the roosts only to be pushed off again by the red ones. We finally shut the door on them and let them have it out.

I don't know who slept on the roosts that first night, but we heard fussing in the chicken house long past chicken bedtime.

Gradually our hens learned to live together, but it took a long time.

The main topic of conversation at church the next Sunday was our chickens. How those farm people loved to tease!

"Hey, Preacher, have your chickens learned to live together yet?" or, "Just like a man and his wife, Preacher, you got to get to know one another before you can get along."

"Had your first fight with your new wife, Preacher?" And they would wink at me.

They knew chickens. They knew people. They knew newlyweds.

Through the years my husband would use our chicken story when he counseled with couples before their marriage. And he often used them to illustrate a sermon on how to get along with neighbors.

Then came the day when we got the telephone call—my mother was seriously ill. Could we come right away to be with her?

In an hour we were packed and ready to leave. Then we remembered—who would take care of our chickens? My husband stepped to the old-fashioned party line telephone and gave two long rings, which meant "everybody listen".

"This is the preacher," he said into the mouthpiece. "We have to be gone a week because of an emergency. Could someone take care of our chickens? And please keep the eggs for your trouble."

"Sure," chorused a dozen voices. "Don't worry," said one. "God keep you—we'll keep your chickens," said another with humor. We left with lighter hearts.

When we got home we found our chickens well cared for and all the eggs neatly packaged in our refrigerator. Our friends knew we had been trading extra eggs to the grocer for bread and milk, so they wouldn't take our eggs.

When we asked around who had fed and watered our chickens, we always got the same answer: "Oh, several people did." We never knew exactly who had helped, but we did know the heartwarming feeling that comes when others care in your time of trouble.

We spent many a pleasant hour that first year watching the antics of our chickens. We talked to them, petted them, scolded them when they were naughty. I would be embarrassed to admit this, except that I know a great many other people do the same things.

We learned that it is the little things in life, simple pleasures along the way, that make us content.

My husband has been the minister for many other churches since then.

We've had a happy life together. We like to think it is because we got such a good beginning with our rural friends and our chickens.

Why am I so reminiscent today? I guess it is because this is our 30th wedding anniversary, and our son and his wife came to see us this afternoon. They brought us a gift—a box of 30 little peeping baby chicks. "To help you remember," they said.

You see, they know the chicken story, too.

CLUCKING, preening, murmuring little chicken secrets...laying hens are like a lot of people in some ways. And that's why they're nice to have around.

Ode To My Cookbook

My cookbook was a gift on the day I was wed,
A 30-year testimony of a family well fed.
The pages are sticky with ingredients devoured;
The cover is frayed, greased and well-floured.

I marked all the recipes that brought fame to me,
Cakes and cookies served at each social tea.
"Too dry", "too moist", "serves five and not 10"—
The data's all there, the where and the when!

There's a note from one child or another—
"I have gone skating with Nick and his brother."
A fourth-grade math paper is marked 92;
We mixed multiplication tables along with the stew.

"Hi, Mom!" simply stated and meant in affection
Is written on a page in the candy section.
Small hands scribbled while they "helped bake"
Or played in pie dough or stirred the cake.

Altitude adjustments and suggested brand names
Blend well with the traces of ticktacktoe games.
A news clipping marks the dessert section for me;
It says the last child has received her degree!

My cookbook, my diary, scrapbook and guide;
With it I coped, baked, roasted or fried!
The book now lies open at "Cooking for Two".
It's a challenge, but one I am glad to pursue!

—Bethene Larson of Cody, Wyoming

These Hands Have Tender Strength

By *Katie Keehner of Monona, Iowa*

The hour is late, I am tired but still wide awake. It has been a long and hard, yet fulfilling day, working beside the man I love more than life itself.

I lie here in the lamplight, one of his tanned and callused hands held in mine. As I trace the deep lines etched into the palm, I see the character they represent.

Wide, bronzed and strong, they can thread on duals, hoist tractor weights, lift 55-gallon oil drums, hitch, unhitch and lift the impossible.

They carry a permanent stain of grease under the fingernails from machinery that is too stubborn to run smoothly, needing the final touch only his nimble fingers can produce.

I have seen these same rough and callused hands reach out and hold two tiny hands with firm gentleness, giving encouragement and love, steadiness and laughter.

These hands are capable of wondrous things! They can steady a bicycle "just so", while small, determined legs gleefully struggle with balance and pedals.

I've watched these hands spank bottoms, pluck out splinters, wipe away tears and gingerly test small, but growing muscles, proudly displayed by two grinning sons.

These hands have wrestled angry sows, delivered, ever-so-gently, a newborn calf, settled my snorting, spooky mare and carefully removed those thorns from puppy's paw.

These giant hands represent a giant heart! They can fix anything, from a combine engine to my kitchen fan and a tearful son's toy.

One hand, that can hold at least eight eggs all the way to the house without one single crack, is the same hand that drives a tenpenny nail all the way in, with only three whacks!

These same, weathered hands, on many a night, have rubbed small, achy feet and taken away the pain only a very young cowboy knows at the end of a day on the ranch.

My man's hands, not so long ago, held mine tightly for hours on end while I struggled with death. His hands were my anchor in swirling waters, my lifeline on a black, stormy sea, my cable of strength.

As I lie here beside him, I know that no matter what may befall me throughout the day, his hands, softly on my shoulders at night, will wipe away all my fear and anxieties. They bring peace to my heart, and I thank God they are mine to hold—cracks, calluses and all!

ONE HAND *can hold at least eight eggs all the way to the house; it's the same hand that drives a tenpenny nail all the way in with just three whacks!*

Everybody Loved Aunt Nanny's Peonies

By Jean Foster of Warrensburg, Ohio

Aunt Nanny's peonies always bloomed in time for Decoration Day.

She loved those peonies, or so it seemed to me. She donned her outdated sunbonnet ("Because it was my mother's," she explained), and ushered me into her flower garden for my yearly introduction to her peony blossoms, nodding heavily on their too-slender stems.

"They'll be beautiful on the graves," she'd muse. "I'm going to take them to the cemetery Sunday." Then we'd proceed row by row past her peony bushes weighted with huge flowers that opened in layers of petals.

She gave me their names, but fortunately she didn't test my memory later. I liked the large pink ones best, though Aunt Nanny loved the reds, yellows, whites and pinks all alike.

When Decoration Day came, Dad packed the shovel, the rake, hand tools and cans for flowers into the trunk of our car.

Mother packed a basket of fried chicken, potato salad, a yellow cabbage-Jello salad and my favorite chocolate cake for our picnic meal at the cemetery. It was a family day, a day of remembering those who were already "across the river", as Mother said, "who are waiting for us".

Aunt Nanny cut the stems of her beautiful blossoms and filled huge containers in the trunk and back seat of the car. Around and between these she stuffed empty cans and Ball glass jars.

Carefully, slowly, she drove to the cemetery at the edge of town, parked by the stone entrance and opened her trunk. People on their way to decorate graves, and even some who were not, stopped to buy her peonies, hear their names and legends and receive a jar or can filled with flowers.

I always thought her pink peonies would be the nicest on Aunt Edith's grave, but Dad insisted on red and yellow. "She always liked lots of color," he'd say.

Aunt Edith was his sister, who died of some mysterious ailment when she was 20 years old, several years before I was even born. Mother said Aunt Edith died in Dad's arms, and that Dad cried a lot over her. I thought a lot about that, and I held the scene in my imagination until I began to believe I had seen it myself.

"You're a lot like Edith," Dad told me often. And believe me, I thought a lot about that, too.

When the tombstones were washed and when Aunt Nanny's peonies graced them all, our family of four had our picnic dinner. There among the headstones that proclaimed BUROKER and STEPHENS, I felt a part of a much larger family. As I ate I tried to memorize the names I read around me, for if we were to meet one day, as Mother insisted, I certainly didn't want to feel like a complete stranger among them.

When Aunt Nanny's peonies were almost sold, she'd walk about the cemetery putting the rest of her flowers in jars and setting the bouquets on the graves of people whose families had not come to decorate and remember.

"There!" she'd say, her eyes filling with unshed tears, her smile curving nearly up to her ears.

Once—and only once—I protested. "But, Aunt Nanny! They're all gone now! All those blooms you love so much!" It seemed almost too much to bear just thinking of her "over 100 at least" peony bushes bereft of their color.

She looked down at me, puzzled at my lack of understanding. "Honey, the peonies are for Decoration Day! They're not for me!"

Puzzled, I tried to sort it all out, to make sense of Aunt Nanny's dedication to raising peonies for one special day. She squeezed my hand. I knew she was happy, for I could feel joy vibrating through her hand into mine. I looked at my parents contentedly sitting on an old quilt near their families' graves.

Something greater than the moment, greater than trimming the graves and washing

50

the tombstones, and even greater than Aunt Nanny's peonies, settled into my mind and became a permanent part of my consciousness. Life and death, I felt sure, were both part of the great good of the universe.

I didn't understand my new-found truth at the time, nor do I fully understand it now. No matter. It's the feeling that counts, the feeling that Aunt Nanny had when she cut her precious peony blossoms to be placed on the graves on Decoration Day.

It's the feeling my parents had when they spent that special afternoon among the graves of their families. It's the feeling I had when I read the names of those who had "gone before". It's a feeling that chases away superstition, fear of the unknown and somehow satisfies the question of "Why?"

A Lifetime of Tenderness Shows in Her Hands

By Berna Dean Kofoot of St. Ansgar, Iowa

Mother's hands aren't much to look at. Her fingers are crooked from arthritis. Her veins stand out, blue and large, like rivers on a map. The skin looks loose and wrinkled, the nails short. But Mom's hands are hands of beauty. Beautiful from years of service to others. I'm holding them as we gaze out across the fields from our chairs here on the porch.

These hands were gentle as she tended her baby. They have carried buckets of water for her family's use, scrubbed clothes and floors, and cooked countless meals. They have given a baby chick its first drink and taught a baby calf to suck.

These hands have delivered baby pigs and felt the pressure as the sow strained. They've worked the garden soil, toiled to produce vegetables, fruit and flowers. They've created beauty year after year with artfully arranged bouquets of flowers.

Mom's hands have kneaded loaves and loaves of bread, and made the largest angel food cakes from scratch. They've made countless quilts (flower garden, wedding ring and nine patch), the stitches small and dainty.

These hands daily fold in prayer as she thanks God for the chance to serve. Yes, Mom's hands are hands of service to others. They are a farm wife's working hands. To me, they are beautiful.

THERE'S joy in living and working in partnership with nature, and a farm woman's hands are willing, working, caring hands.

She Left a Legacy
Of Love and Pepper Relish

By Betty Jane Hewitt of Newton Falls, Ohio

This was a good season for peppers. I made Bertha's red pepper relish this morning, and the kitchen steamed up bright and tangy, just like hers used to.

Bertha was special to me, although I knew her more as an acquaintance than a close friend. She took great pride in being a farmer's wife, working alongside her husband on their dairy farm and taking care of her family and her garden.

She was happiest cooking for friends and family, and for years we could never have a successful church supper without her. I was washing dishes in the church kitchen after one of these dinners when I first tasted her pepper relish.

Aunt Bertha raised beautiful flowers. Not the exotic kind, just rows and rows of tulips, daffodils and iris in the spring. Her yard was full of glads, peonies, zinnias and larkspur in the summer and mums in the fall. How delighted she would be that our church sanctuary is graced with two tall brass urns, arranged with brilliant flowers—in her memory.

Bertha's legacy to me is knowing the contentment in the beauty and goodness of a backyard garden, a feeling she must have experienced often after days and weeks of hard work with her flowers and vegetables. For her, contentment, was being herself, come mistakes, problems, heartbreak or whatever.

Can you find immortality in red pepper relish? Each fall I grind red and green peppers and onions, and the sweet, biting smell of spices and vinegar simmering on the stove wafts through the house.

It's then that I really remember Bertha... and I am glad.

His Hands
Have Quiet, Loving Strength

By Marjory Scheufler of Belpre, Kansas

Have I really been married all these years to that man sleeping there in the recliner? One of his sun-browned hands folded across his chest shows the skinned knuckle he got on the chute when we worked cattle yesterday.

He's so quiet. First time today I've seen him stopped. The worried frown is gone from his forehead. It will soon be time to wake him for the 10 o'clock news and weather. That frown will be back when he hears the storm is supposed to be worse than expected. It's so cold. Sure hope he doesn't need me to help him get that cow in the barn.

How much he has changed in these past years. From the tall, painfully thin, serious, intense, driving young man that I married to this still thin, very trim, somewhat mellowed, and better looking with age, absolute farmer.

How does he do it? He keeps the checkbook balance in his head. Can figure creages, board feet, hundredweights and bushels in the same way.

He can see a cow in trouble across the pasture, the tire tread of vehicles that drive in the yard and identify the owner. The storm clouds when they first come up in the southwest and through me in an instant.

He gets so darned mad at me because I don't run fast enough to cut off the bull as he runs for the heifer switching her tail enticingly over the hill. Or, when I jerk the chain too hard anytime I'm the puller.

Then he'll pat me on the rear and smile 'cause I held the bolt just right in the wee small place on the combine that he couldn't get into with his bigger hand.

I've had to acknowledge the fact that this land is his mistress. She is more demanding, enticing, mysterious and unpredictable than I could ever be.

I don't try to compete, because he's not even aware of his first love. She's just there and always has been.

Thirty years on this farm, in this house with this man. Raised five kids with him. Did you know I still get that little thrill with his touch? Dear God, how I love him and this place in time.

Her Love Lives On In All of Us

By Elaine Taylor of Ozark, Missouri

Aunt Bird died this morning. I am so glad I had the opportunity to talk with her and to tell her I loved her the day she got the news about the cancer spreading.

I remember so clearly her saying "Don't forget what Uncle Oscar taught you." What he taught me was to love God and our fellow man, to do good and live peaceably.

Uncle Oscar and Aunt Bird had just about the most perfect marriage I've ever seen. It lasted over 50 years with God in the center. Having no children of their own—their only daughter died at birth—they loved and shared what they had with many nieces, nephews, and great-nephews and -nieces.

A favorite and typical memory of mine is one of spending 2 or 3 days with Aunt Bird and Uncle Oscar on their farm in the summer. The old house was amply shaded by big trees and surrounded by flowers. The trees were *grand* for climbing and swaying in the wind!

No one ever said, "Get down. You'll get hurt." If anything was said, it was likely to be "How's the weather up there?" as Uncle Oscar grinned up through the leafy branches, as he relaxed for a few minutes after dinner in a lawn chair.

The fact that all water came from the well close by the back door didn't faze Aunt Bird when it came to having guests. Whether her company was a small niece, a crowd of relatives for Christmas, or the minister and his wife, she provided delicious meals.

Skillet cornbread was an everyday dish in the summer. Gooseberry and pecan pies were baked for special meals.

Water glasses were always filled with a dipper from the water bucket which sat just inside the kitchen door. After a meal was over, all hot water for dishwashing was heated in a teakettle.

And sharing the living water from God's word was just as much an everyday occurrence as carrying water from the well.

At night, just before bedtime, Aunt Bird and Uncle Oscar would both sit down in the living room for a quiet devotional time. Uncle Oscar would read a passage from the Bible. Aunt Bird might read something aloud from a Christian magazine. After a prayer it was off to bed for all of us.

Their deep love for each other and for God was their gift to me. Through their example,

I have tried to build a good strong marriage. My husband and I read the Bible every night. We are trying to teach our sons to be thankful in all things, as the scripture teaches.

Today, after she died, I realized more fully that the influence from Aunt Bird and Uncle Oscar will live on. Today at lunch our 4-year-old son asked to say the blessing. Bowing his head and in a happy voice he said "Thank you, God, for the pretty day—for taking Aunt Bird to heaven. And for the food..."

Yes, Aunt Bird died this morning, but her loving influence will live on for many generations to come.

She Had Her Eye On Farmer for a Beau

By Carolyn Owens of Edina, Minnesota

Once, when I was young and spry, a handsome stranger caught my eye. He had it all—looks youth and charm. To top it off, he owned a farm.

I made my plans and acted coy, to capture that unknowing boy.

My darling never stood a chance, and soon we danced our wedding dance.

Fifty years gone since that day—my, how time has slipped away.

Think back now in good fun, with just a hint of a smile: Before he had a chance to run, I ran him down the aisle!

Life Goes On, And That's Just Beautiful

By Lila Allen of Reno, Nevada

Today I am a widow. Yesterday I was a wife. I stand out on the porch in the morning sun, my favorite place for a coffee break. The memories are good here, the thoughts positive. I sip my coffee and look at the clean sweep of the ranch out over the valley and up to the pine-studded mountains, the cattle scattered ut in contented grazing.

Today I think alone. Yesterday I shared
my thoughts. I hear the gate chain drop at the
road. I look up and see her running up the lane,
her dark hair shining in the early-morning sun.
She stumbles and picks herself up as only a
-year-old can do.

Today is every day. Yesterday was always
tomorrow—plans made by two for two, not to be
done by one.

My son had said, "Come, Mom, stay with
us, we have a little ray of sunshine at our
house." But running to or from does not allow
adjustment, so I stayed in our home. I've gone to
theirs many times, though, and felt the welcomed
love there and soaked up the warmth of that
little ray of sunshine.

She stops to pick a flower, a child
enchanted by nature's beauty.

Today is. Today I must plan for tomorrow. Today I do think of the yesterdays, but I
must concentrate on today and all the tomorrows
to be.

And when I find myself suddenly caught
up in the planning of moving my home to the
small bit of land set aside for retirement years, I
become enthused. A wee sunbeam follows me as
I go, clutching my hand as we explore my new
little corner of the world—the new spring plants
there, wild, plentiful and ready to share this
world with me. I find plans made by two can be
done by one.

She swings the yard gate open and steps
just inside.

"Grandma, look at the pretty new
flowler'," she chirps. She squats beside a new
pansy and gently strokes its soft little face.

Then as she comes along by the porch
and lifts her dimpled cherub face and looks at me
through sparkly blue eyes framed in dark lashes,
a lovely butterfly flutters near.

"Oh, Grandma, such a pretty butterfly!"
she sighs.

Today I am a woman, surrounded by love
of my family, close enough to share but far
enough away to allow me to be myself.

She comes up the steps, and I kneel down
to welcome the open arms that wrap around my
neck. I feel the surge of joy as I hear,
"Grandma, I love you."

Today I am not alone.

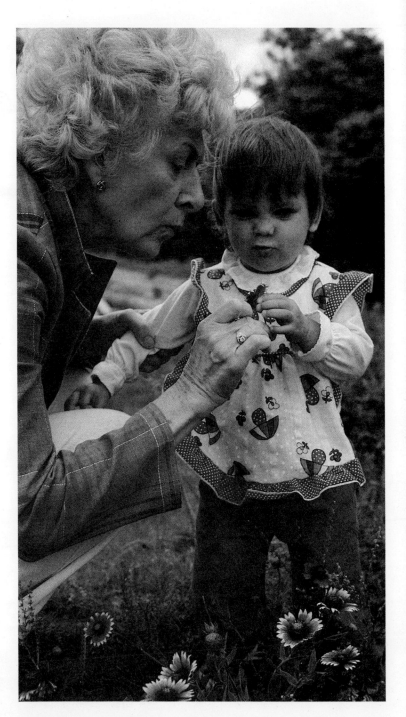

GRANDMAS *and granddaughters
have a special bond of tenderness
between them...and that's
just how it should be.*

4

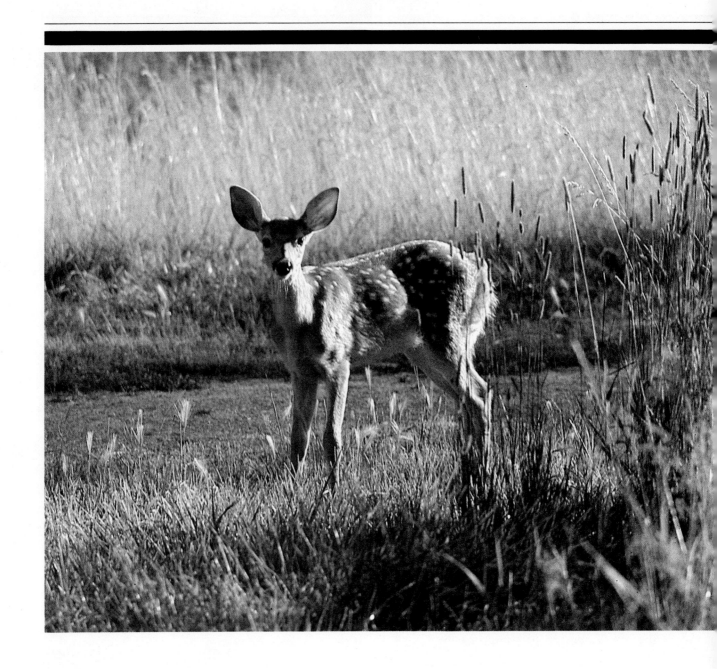

Nature at My Doorstep
Songs of Country Beauty

Will the Swallows Come Back To Clark's Dairy?

By Rosalie Clark of Moulton, Alabama

The "Empty Nest Syndrome", a term coined in medical circles to describe the symptoms middle-aged women exhibit at the loss of their children, has come to have a literal, yet more profound meaning for me.

I stare at the empty bird nest lying on a newspaper atop my desk. The nest measures about 8 in. across. The exposed side is coated with a dry mud shell hard as stucco, while the inside is whirled straw lined with down.

A fleeting sense of sadness comes over me as I look at it. Does it represent the swift passage of time, the neglect of too much beauty or perhaps a sorrow that my own babies have flown?

Spring is a busy time on a dairy farm, so we didn't notice the birds on our front porch until the nest was almost complete. I opened the front door to let in a little April sunshine, and there it was perched on a ledge in front of the glass storm door.

"They've already made about all the mess they will," my husband, Travis, said. "We might as well leave them until the little ones hatch."

With both birds sharing the egg-warming chores, it was a while before we could climb up to count them. There were four ecru-colored ovals, darkly freckled with brown.

Soon everybody who came by showed an interest in the birds. Travis, whose pretty accurate nature lore has been handed down through generations of farmers, called them barn swallows because of the forked tail and swooping flight. But I, whose love of nature began when I read the works of naturalists Edwin Way Teale and Roger Tory Peterson, had to prove it by a book.

The illustration threw me off. The colors were much too vivid. Our birds were not dark blue, but gray; the throat a faint blush, not bright red; the underparts light gray, not salmon. But I put this down as artistic license when I read the description. Barn swallows are common to our Tennessee Valley region, migrate farther south in winter, love to be near water (our pond), nest in buildings (usually deserted) and live entirely off insects caught in flight.

What a boon for our garden! For years without success, I had been lobbying for martin boxes.

Then one day around the first of May, Travis came in as excited as if one of our Holsteins had won a blue ribbon at the county fair. "The swallows hatched!" he exclaimed, holding up a crumpled half of speckled eggshell. "I wanted to know how many, but when I tried to check, the mother bird swooped at me."

"At you?" I countered, looking at his 6-ft.

AS SURE as spring, barn swallows on a country place are another symbol of life's constant cycles. And wouldn't we miss them swooping here and there?

frame.

"Oh, she didn't really get close, but swallows do threaten. Last year when I was plowing the corn, a couple of crows got too near a nest, and the swallows attacked and actually drove the crows away though they were three times as big."

After that we didn't stay on the front porch more than a few minutes at a time, because the parent birds became agitated and left off feeding the young, which was almost continual. The parents made trip after trip, stopping on a nearby ledge to visibly pant now and again.

As the birds grew we could see four open mouths, visible above the edge of the nest. They hungrily jerked their heads back when the door opened, so we got to peeping through the glass door at them.

Our earlier optimism about the mess proved false. Travis noticed, "The little birds never foul their nest. They always hang over the side."

"Goody for them and *their* house," I answered sarcastically, looking at the pile of droppings on the concrete below, the streaks on the column in between. We decided, like so much in life, everything depends on the viewpoint.

One Sunday when our married children were home we noticed our bird family also had visitors. "Just neighbors dropping in to see the new babies," Paul guessed.

"Probably the grandparents coming in to help feed all those hungry mouths," snorted Travis.

"Ha," laughed Linda, leaning down to 3-month-old Daniel. "You see how your grandpa's mind works."

Finally we noticed late one afternoon the parent birds were teaching a young one to fly while the remaining three jammed together, bright eyes shining. "They'll probably be gone in a few days," we said. The next morning the nest was empty.

I left the nest for a few weeks half in hope the swallows would raise another family, but now the painter is coming to give our house trim a new coat. Since the nest had to come down, I pared it off the inside cornice with a dull butcher knife.

Still we have learned to appreciate one more species of nature's creatures a little better. Now when we drive the pickup around the farm at dusk, we stop to watch the flocks of swallows dive in their never-ending quest for food, their movements graceful as ballerinas. I reflect that the God whose eye is on the sparrow must love them, too.

The book said swallows often return to the same nesting location each year. I forget the litter and think only of the pleasure they brought. Just as my grandchildren have cured my "Empty Nest Syndrome", so another hatch of swallows might cure my nostalgia over these.

Morning Starlight Softens a Harsh Mood

By Frances Armstrong of Ponca, Nebraska

Life holds some special moments for each person—a marriage, a birth, a rekindled friendship, or perhaps a hundred other treasured memories.

There are also lesser events which are remembered because of their beauty.

By the way of explanation, let me say I married a farmer and let me add it was clearly understood that I married not only the man but also his way of life. His cows, pigs, horses, his weeds and crops were suddenly part and parcel of my life.

A separate career of my own? It seemed

nthinkable. Plenty of time for my own needs nd fulfillment? Well, now!

Unquestioningly, I rearranged my think-ng and my daily routine to fit the needs of the man and the beasts. Did I like it? Well, hardly, ut I loved the man.

One morning, in the cold February arkness, I sat on a one-legged stool in the barn milking gentle old Bess. You could relax with old ess. She always stood still.

As I milked, my mind wandered, ponder-ng my fate and marveling at how love had rought me to this barn and this early morning outine.

My spirits were sagging. But as I walked to the house, suddenly the whole world about me was filled with a bright celestial light.

I raised my eyes skyward, wondering if my time had come, and blazing across the sky was a falling star, so close it seemed I could almost reach it.

Its trail of fire was so beautifully long and glorious, I was transfixed. And then in an instant it was gone.

But not really. For although old Bess is long gone and little remains of those days but memories, I can still close my eyes and see a marvel—a wonder that lifted me above the mun-dane world to beauty so ethereal it still remains in my memory.

Take Time—
Enjoy Life's Glories

By Shirley Harvey of Barre, Vermont

There's a beautiful lilac bush at the corner of our porch, and every spring I plan to ake one whole afternoon and sit on the porch doing nothing but smelling the lilacs.

But spring is a busy time around our place and the lilacs bloom for only a very short time.

Then someone comes walking around the porch and says "too bad your lilacs are gone, hey were so lovely." And I regretfully think—another spring has come and gone and I didn't have time to enjoy the lilacs!

How many of the beautiful things of life do we let pass by because we do not take time to enjoy them while we have the opportunity? Why is it that we find time to clean the closets, but not time to smell the lilacs?

In the Bible, we read the story of Mary and Martha. While Martha was "cumbered about by much serving", Mary sat at the Savior's feet, listening to Him. She instinctively knew this was the most important thing in her world at the moment.

When Martha complained to Jesus that

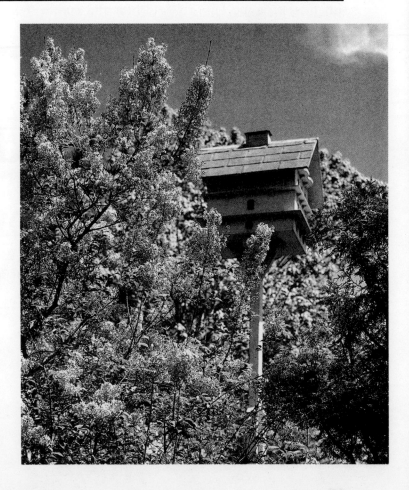

Mary had left her to serve alone, He told her Mary had chosen the "better part" which should not be taken from her. Are we always careful to choose "the better part"?

Some memory-making times come only once in our lives. And if we don't take advantage of them when they come they are soon gone.

I remember one occasion when our son was 4 years old. He came rushing into the house wide-eyed and wanted me to come *right now* to see the big chipmunk he was chasing. I dropped the dish towel and went. (That was one time I was *especially* glad I did—his "big chipmunk" turned out to be a skunk.)

When a child first notices that the big, round moon in the sky has turned into something that resembles a banana, it's fun to see the expression on his face.

And you don't want to miss your daughter's first rainbow! You watch her drink in the beauty of the glistening colors against the gray sky, and the marvels of this beautiful world are new again in your eyes. Rainbows don't wait until you have finished vacuuming!

I often see a tiny baby with a bottle propped up beside him in the crib because his mother is too busy to hold him and cuddle him while he eats.

My chipmunk-chasing son now rides a motorcycle and plays hockey, and I cherish all the times I held and cuddled him while he was just a little guy.

There are good reasons to pause and enjoy the beautiful things of life. A recent survey by the National Institute of Mental Health show two factors—nutrition and environment— contribute to mental illness.

Living in a tension-filled environment and always racing against the clock without taking time to "recharge" contributes to mental illness for ourselves and our children. We can even assimilate our food better in a calm, relaxed atmosphere.

We shouldn't feel guilty when we pause to enjoy some of the beauties of nature. What tranquilizer could be better than listening to a pitter-patter of rain on the roof?

This world was created for us to experience and enjoy, and if we crowd our lives with so much that we can't enjoy the things which bring us fulfillment and make us happier people, we miss a great deal.

Smelling lilacs or watching a rainbow may not be your "thing", but whatever is "choosing the better part" for you should be what you find time to do. Remember—rainbows don't wait.

Each Dawn Holds Promise For the Future

By Diane Lane of Wilson, New York

There's frost on the young alfalfa stem. Teardrop diamonds glisten on the spiderweb, as the early morning sun rises enthusiastically, vibrantly, from behind the trees to the east.

I've known for several minutes that dawn is coming as I've stood here on the porch, breathing in the air that is sweet, moist and faintly cool to my nostrils.

A swallow, up from the cliffs by the lake, darts sharply in front of my view, and the redwing blackbird trills the notes I've waited all winter to hear.

Life in the spring to me seems a promise each day from nature that life renews itself and is only better each year. From my cloistered spot on the farm I find it hard to believe that air pollution could possibly make my morning sunrise redder than last year. How could fly ash be responsible for making the spider's web more pronounced? Life here seems far too free, lovely

…d eternal, even in its cycles, to ever come to … end.

There is so much that is grand here. I …ow there are other meadows with deer and …easants. The sun shines as magnificently 5 …inutes down the road from us. But, to me, …ere is no place like our farm for a familiar feast …all that is good, wholesome, everlasting and …ue to its created purpose.

I really feel this morning like I am part of a small earthly kingdom, not in a political sense but in the grand scheme of things. This is a spring morning that makes me feel that there is time for everything and a season for all my dreams.

IN THE COUNTRY, *the senses don't have to compete with man's structures and noises to feel the absolute beauty all around.*

*"I am deeply impressed and duly inspired by the painted panorama
I am witnessing, as the beauty of this spectacular change is being stamped
in the recesses of my memory..."*

Bittersweet Autumn Cannot Linger

By Bernice Maddux of Weatherford, Texas

As I stand in the section of nature's revolving door allotted to autumn, there's a promise to myself I intend to keep. It's a promise to take a long and careful look this time, to see if autumn really is as special, spectacular and spontaneous as I remember.

As I watch autumn critically, the first characteristic I observe is that she seems to be a bit of an introvert when it comes to getting her way. I am in sympathy.

Summer—like a sultry tenant whose lease has expired but won't move out—pulls stubbornly at autumn, encouraging her to be hot and humid, a carbon copy of her predecessor.

On the other side winter taunts, frequently stepping over the dividing line to preview his chilly demands that autumn be bold, cold and blustery.

Instead of defiantly defending her rights to be herself and not wanting to hurt either's feelings, autumn gives in to one and then the other, meekly snatching only a day or two here and there to do her own thing.

Awed and inspired by autumn's flurry of transition, I feel her changes as if I were leaving the hot, fumy freeways for the quiet cool of the open country.

Observing autumn's rather erratic behavior, I, too, seem to be in a state of limbo. I have finally escaped scorched and weary from summer and am not yet a captive of winter. I coast and dream during this most deserved intermission, my memory photographing the season's haunting beauty for future reference.

Autumn definitely has a way with color, a fact that I had vividly remembered, but am reconfirming daily for my own pleasure. Under her watchful eye, trees sift their variegated leaves of yellow, orange, red and brown through a frisky breeze. They flutter and dance to the faded grass below.

Heartier flowers still can be seen lounging in the golden moments, as if in no special hurry to depart. There is not so much competition now, and their sturdy beauty is contested only by the gold of ripening grain and the orange shared equally by the maturing pumpkins and persimmons.

Autumn is a busy time. As I pause to look above the potpourri of color surrounding me, I gaze into hazy skies of blue silk to see geese flying in formation.

On cue from Mother Nature, they are southward bound. Complying with the migratory message, there is no turning back; we will see no more of them for a long while. Realizing this, I watch until they are no more.

While man gathers his harvest, there is big business afoot in the animal world, too, as it prepares for the long and icy ravages of deepening winter.

Not in the least disturbed by my presence, the frolic-some squirrel makes countless, hurried trips to his hole high in the oak with his growing cargo of nuts. He stops and scolds me briefly for doing nothing. He would not understand that I, too, am busy—busy observing. It is important work.

I am deeply impressed and duly inspired by the painted panorama I am witnessing, as the beauty of this spectacular change is being

...amped in the recesses of my memory. How rare ...sight this is!

I silently thank the sturdy oaks, still ...anding in the woodlands fully clothed, ...ng after less-determined trees have re-linquished their colorful coats.

Now I remember vividly what is so great about autumn. I realize sadly that she will be gone long before I am ready, and I shall mourn her passing.

Each Month Is Rare and Precious

by Marlyce Peterson of Willow Lake, South Dakota

Pink sunrises shivering against the white horizon...bird tracks that look like blanket ...titches in the snow...lighting a new candle and ...hispering a prayer...these are January.

February is giant drifts of snow enticing ...hildren to play "Fox and Goose". A Valentine ...ith "I love you Mom" shines on a steamy ...itchen window. The sky wears pink cheeks and ...olden tresses as she kisses a white world good ...ight.

Crocuses are silently stretching in March. ...miles are silly lines holding up my heart. The ...norning sky, like a young ballerina, dances in on ...ink toes. Flying geese are honking, "Welcome, ...pring!"

In April a red geranium sits on my ...indowsill. Rain splashes, then races down the ...indow pane. April is buds bursting on the trees. ...ound a brown field rabbit and batch of kittens ...oday. Frost crept in while we were sleeping, but ...ow the morning sun wraps warm arms around ...he earth, embracing her.

May whispers love notes through the ...reezes. A red-headed pheasant and a gopher ...tand up and wink at me! Prayer is refreshment ...or the soul. I smell lilacs, pick rhubarb and plant ...ny garden. May, I love you.

The garden is my chapel in June. Barefoot ...ids find warm rain puddles. Old lace curtains ...illow out the broken window of a deserted farm-...ouse as I pick yellow roses by the gate. Sunrise ...narks a new beginning. Sunset is the benediction ...or a closing day.

In July the hay is down and the rain is hiding behind a low dark cloud. Hollyhocks wave like can-can dancers. A deer plays hide and seek in the rye field. My hubby surprises me by giving me a butterfly, a touch of beauty and inner joy.

August—a quick summer shower and rainbow. If I were an angel, I'd use the rainbow for a giant slide! Now is a time of harvest and long, hot days. I oversleep and find the sun riding on a cloud. Heat penetrates the sky and leaves it a burnt umber. Crickets talk and talk! A walk among my roses is a processional to the morning.

It's September, and I wonder where the summer has gone. I tuck a prayer in my pocket and start a new day. The moon is riding on inky, dark clouds. Gardens yield in abundance. Those who toil respect their labor. Autumn's shawl is slipping over summer's pleasant hours.

October is autumn leaves wearing fruit-wood sandals and whirling, orange-chiffon gowns. Hundreds of blackbirds high in the treetops are singing an autumn serenade. Geese pattern the sky, honk and wave good-bye, and I'm left behind. Even if I was blind, I could feel these seasons.

November comes in with a rainstorm and leaves a shimmering, sparkling, ice-covered world. A few brown leaves remain on skeleton trees. The day ends cold and gray, and the wind wraps itself into my dreams.

December is cold winds with sharp and brittle breath. My window pane paints a fairy-land of trees covered with silver white frost. Behind them stretches a blue-velvet sky. The clothesline looks like stretched taffy. God pulls the shade of twilight, and darkness fills my world for another day. It's time to rest.

Spring in the Garden

Ruth Hale Woodside of Hyde Park, Vermont

As she bends her back to spring's fresh earth,
I think of two weddings, a death and a birth
that our town has shared since last she hoed
her little garden by that dirt road.

She's never seen the city's sights,
the teeming traffic, those flashing lights...
but all of life has touched her here—
she has known love, sadness and fear.

Her husband's "gone", her children have flown—
but she carries within the love she has known.
She looks to the sky as she hears a bird sing
and plants in her garden, the joy of spring.